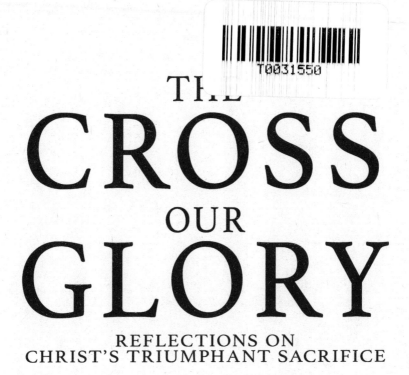

THE CROSS OUR GLORY

REFLECTIONS ON
CHRIST'S TRIUMPHANT SACRIFICE

CHARLES H.
SPURGEON

WHITAKER
HOUSE

THE CROSS, OUR GLORY
Reflections on Christ's Triumphant Sacrifice

ISBN: 979-8-88769-136-7
eBook ISBN: 979-8-88769-137-4
Printed in the United States of America
© 2024 by Whitaker House

Whitaker House
1030 Hunt Valley Circle
New Kensington, PA 15068
www.whitakerhouse.com

Library of Congress Control Number: 2023952243

CONTENTS

THE CROSS, OUR GLORY

Almost all men have something in which to glory. Every bird has its own note of song. It is a poor heart that never rejoices. It is a dull packhorse that is altogether without bells. Men usually rejoice in something or other, and many men so rejoice in that which they choose that they become boastful and full of vainglory. It is very sad that men should be ruined by their glory, and yet many are. Many glory in their shame, and more glory in that which is mere emptiness. Some glory in their physical strength, in which an ox excels them; or in their gold, which is but thick clay; or in their gifts, which are but talents with which they are entrusted. The pounds entrusted to their stewardship are thought, by men, to belong to themselves, and, therefore, they rob God of the glory of them. O my hearers, hear the voice of Wisdom, which cries, "He that glories, let him glory only in the Lord." To live for personal glory is to be dead while we live! Be not so foolish as to perish for a bubble! Many a man has thrown his soul away for a little honor or for the transient satisfaction of success in trifles. O men, your tendency is to glory in something—your wisdom will be to find a glory worthy of an immortal mind!

—Charles H. Spurgeon

I

GETHSEMANE

"And being in an agony He prayed more earnestly:
and His sweat was as it were great drops of blood falling
down to the ground."
—Luke 22:44

Few had fellowship with the sorrows of Gethsemane. The majority of the disciples were not there. They were not sufficiently advanced in grace to be admitted to behold the mysteries of "the agony." Occupied with the Passover feast at their own houses, they represent the many who live upon the letter but are mere babes and sucklings as to the spirit of the gospel. The walls of Gethsemane fitly typify that weakness in grace which effectually shuts in the deeper marvels of communion from the gaze of ordinary believers. To twelve, nay, to eleven only was the privilege given to enter Gethsemane and see this great sight. Out of the eleven, eight were left at some distance; they had fellowship, but not of that intimate sort to which the men greatly beloved are admitted. Only three highly favored ones, who had been with Him on the mount of transfiguration (see Matthew 17:1–13) and had witnessed the life-giving miracle in the house of Jairus (see Mark 5:37–43)— only these three could approach the veil of His mysterious sorrow:

within that veil even these must not intrude; a stone's-cast distance must be left between. He must tread the winepress alone, and of the people there must be none with Him. Peter and the two sons of Zebedee represent the few eminent, experienced, grace-taught saints who may be written down as "Fathers"; these, having done business on great waters, can, in some degree, measure the huge Atlantic waves of their Redeemer's passion; having been much alone with Him, they can read His heart far better than those who merely see Him amid the crowd. To some selected spirits it is given, for the good of others, and to strengthen them for some future, special, and tremendous conflict, to enter the inner circle and hear the pleadings of the suffering High Priest; they have fellowship with Him in His sufferings and are made conformable unto His death. Yet I say, even these—the elect out of the elect, these choice and peculiar favorites among the King's courtiers— even these cannot penetrate the secret places of the Savior's woe so as to comprehend all His agonies. "Thine unknown sufferings" is the remarkable expression of the Greek liturgy; for there is an inner chamber in His grief, shut out from human knowledge and fellowship. Was it not here that Christ was more than ever an "unspeakable gift" to us? Is not Watts right when he sings—

"And all the unknown joys he gives,
    Were bought with agonies unknown"

Since it would not be possible for any believer, however experienced, to know for himself all that our Lord endured in the place of the olive press, when He was crushed beneath the upper and the nether millstone of mental suffering and hellish malice, it is clearly far beyond the preacher's capacity to set it forth to you. Jesus Himself must give you access to the wonders of Gethsemane; as for me, I can but invite you to enter the garden, bidding you put your shoes from off your feet, for the place whereon we stand is holy ground. I am neither Peter, nor James, nor John, but one who would fain like them drink of the Master's cup and be baptized with His baptism. I have hitherto advanced only so far as yonder band of eight, but there I have listened to the deep groanings of the man of sorrows. Some of you, my venerable friends, may have learned far more than I; but you will not refuse to hear again the roarings of the many waters which strove to quench the love of the Great Husband of our souls.

Several matters will require our brief consideration.

I. THE SAVIOR'S UNUTTERABLE WOE

The emotions of that mournful night are expressed by several words in Scripture. John describes Him as saying, four days before His passion, *"Now is My soul troubled"* (John 12:27). As he marked the gathering clouds, he hardly knew where to turn himself, and cried out, *"What shall I say?"* (John 12:27). Matthew writes of Him, *"He...began to be sorrowful and very heavy"* (Matthew 26:37). Upon the word *ademonein*, translated "very heavy," Goodwin remarks that there was a distraction in the Savior's agony, since the root of the word signifies "separated from the people—men in distraction, being separated from mankind." What a thought, my brethren, that our blessed Lord should be driven to the very verge of distraction by the intensity of His anguish. Matthew represents the Savior Himself as saying, *"My soul is exceeding sorrowful, even to death"* (Matthew 26:38). Here is the word *perilupos*, meaning encompassed, encircled, overwhelmed with grief. "He was plunged head and ears in sorrow and had no breathing-hole" is the strong expression of Goodwin. Sin leaves no cranny for comfort to enter, and therefore the sin-bearer must be entirely immersed in woe. Clark records that He began to be *sore amazed*, and to be very heavy. In this case, *thambeisthai*, with the prefix *ek*, shows extremity of amazement like that of Moses when he did *"exceedingly fear and quake"* (Hebrews 12:21). O blessed Savior, how can we bear to think of Thee as a man astonished and alarmed! Yet was it even so when the terrors of God set themselves in array against Thee. Luke uses the strong language of my text—*"being in an agony"* (Luke 22:44). These expressions, each of them worthy to be the theme of a discourse, are quite sufficient to show that the grief of the Savior was of the most extraordinary character, well justifying the prophetic exclamation *"Behold, and see if there be any sorrow like to my sorrow, which is done to me"* (Lamentations 1:12). He stands before us peerless in misery. None are molested by the powers of evil as He was, as if the powers of hell had given commandment to their legions, *"Fight neither with small nor great, save only with the king of Israel"* (1 Kings 22:31).

Should we profess to understand all the sources of our Lord's agony, wisdom would rebuke us with the question "Have you entered into the springs of the sea? Or have you walked in search of the depths?" (See Job 16:38.) We cannot do more than look at the revealed causes of grief. It partly arose from the horror of His soul *when fully comprehending the meaning of sin.* Brethren, when you were first convinced of sin and saw it as a thing exceeding sinful, though your perception of its sinfulness was but faint compared with its real heinousness, yet horror took hold upon you. Do you remember those sleepless nights? Like the psalmist, you said, *"My bones waxed old through my roaring all the day long. For day and night Your hand was heavy upon me: my moisture is turned into the drought of summer"* (Psalm 32:3–5). Some of us can remember when our souls chose strangling rather than life; when, if the shadows of death could have covered us from the wrath of God, we would have been too glad to sleep in the grave that we might not make our bed in hell. Our blessed Lord saw sin in its natural blackness. He had a most distinct perception of its treasonable assault upon His God, its murderous hatred to Himself, and its destructive influence upon mankind. Well might horror take hold upon Him, for a sight of sin must be far more hideous than a sight of hell, which is but its offspring.

Another deep fountain of grief was found in the fact that Christ now *assumed more fully His official position with regard to sin*. He was now made *sin*. Hear the word! *"He has made Him to be sin for us, who knew no sin; that we might be made the righteousness of God in Him"* (2 Corinthians 5:21). In that night the words of Isaiah were fulfilled: *"The Lord has laid on Him the iniquity of us all"* (Isaiah 53:6). Now He stood as the sin-bearer, the substitute accepted by divine justice to bear, that we might never bear, the whole of wrath divine. At that hour heaven looked on Him as standing in the sinner's stead and treated as sinful man had richly deserved to be treated. Oh! Dear friends, when the immaculate Lamb of God found Himself in the place of the guilty, when He could not repudiate that place because He had voluntarily accepted it in order to save His chosen, what must His soul have felt, how must His perfect nature have been shocked, at such close association with iniquity?

We believe that at this time, *our Lord had a very clear view of all the shame and suffering of His crucifixion*. The agony was but one of the first drops of the tremendous shower which discharged itself upon His head. He foresaw the speedy coming of the traitor-disciple, the seizure by the officers, the mock-trials before the Sanhedrin, and Pilate, and Herod, the scourging and buffeting, the crown of thorns, the shame, and the spitting. All these rose up before His mind, and, as it is a general law of our nature that the foresight of trial is more grievous than trial itself, we can conceive how it was that He who answered not a word when in the midst of the conflict, could not restrain Himself from strong crying and tears in the prospect of it. Beloved friends, if you can revive before your mind's eye the terrible incidents of His death: the hounding through the streets of Jerusalem, the nailing to the cross, the fever, the thirst, and, above all, the forsaking of His God, you cannot marvel that He *"began to be sore amazed, and to be very heavy"* (Mark 14:33).

But possibly a yet more fruitful tree of bitterness was this—*that now His Father began to withdraw His presence from Him.* The shadow of that great eclipse began to fall upon His spirit when He knelt in that cold midnight amidst the olives of Gethsemane. The sensible comforts which had cheered His spirit were taken away; that blessed application of promises which Christ Jesus needed as a man was removed; all that we understand by the term "consolations of God" were hidden from His eyes. He was left single-handed in His weakness to contend for the deliverance of man. The Lord stood by as if He were an indifferent spectator, or, rather, as if He were an adversary, He wounded Him *"with the wound of an enemy, with the chastisement of a cruel one"* (Jeremiah 30:14).

But in our judgment the fiercest heat of the Savior's suffering in the garden lay in *the temptations of Satan.* That hour above any time in His life, even beyond the forty days' conflict in the wilderness, was *the time of his temptation.* "*This is your hour, and the power of darkness*" (Luke 22:53). Now could He emphatically say, "*The prince of this world comes*" (John 14:30). This was His last hand-to-hand fight with all the hosts of hell, and here must He sweat great drops of blood before the victory can be achieved. (See Luke 22:44.)

We have glanced at the fountains of the great deep which were broken up when the floods of grief deluged the Redeemer's soul. Brethren, this one lesson before we pass from the contemplation: "*We have not a high priest which cannot be touched with the feeling of our infirmities; but was in all points tempted like as we are, yet without sin. Let us therefore come boldly to the throne of grace, that we may obtain mercy, and find grace to help in time of need*" (Hebrews 4:15–16). Let us reflect that no suffering can be unknown to Him. We do but run with footmen; He had to contend with horsemen. We do but wade up to our ankles in shallow streams of sorrow; He had to buffet with the swellings of Jordan. He will never fail to succor His people when tempted; even as it was said of old, "*In all their affliction He was afflicted, and the angel of His presence saved them"* (Isaiah 63:9).

II. THE TEMPTATION OF OUR LORD

At the outset of his career, the serpent began to nibble at the heel of the promised deliverer; and now, as the time approached when the seed of the woman should bruise the serpent's head, that old dragon made a desperate attempt upon his great destroyer. It is not possible for us to lift the veil where revelation has permitted it to fall, but we can form some faint idea of the suggestions with which Satan tempted our Lord. Let us, however, remark by way of caution, before we attempt to paint this picture, that whatever Satan may have suggested to our Lord, His perfect nature did not in any degree whatever submit to it so as to sin. The temptations were, doubtless, of the very foulest character, but they left no speck or flaw upon Him, who remained still the fairest among ten thousand. The prince of this world came, but he had nothing in Christ. He struck the sparks, but they did not fall, as in our case, upon dry tinder; they fell as into the sea and were quenched at once. He hurled the fiery arrows, but they could not even scar the flesh of Christ; they smote upon the buckler of His perfectly righteous nature, and they fell off with their points broken, to the discomfiture of the adversary.

But what, think you, were these temptations? It strikes me, from some hints given, that they were somewhat as follows— there was, first, *a temptation to leave the work unfinished*; we may gather this from the prayer *"If it be possible, let this cup pass from Me"* (Matthew 26:39). "Son of God," the tempter said, "is it so? Art Thou really called to bear the sin of man? Hath God said, 'I have laid help upon one that is mighty,' and art Thou He, the chosen of God, to bear all this load? Look at Your weakness! You sweat, even now, great drops of blood; surely You art not He whom the Father has ordained to be mighty to save; or, if You are, what will You win by it? What will it avail You? You have glory enough already. See what miscreants they are for whom You art to offer up Yourself a sacrifice. Your best friends are asleep about You when You need their comfort the most; Your treasurer, Judas, is hastening to betray You for the price of a common slave. The world for which You sacrifice Yourself will cast out Your name as evil, and Your church, for which You do pay the ransom price, what is it worth? A company of mortals! Your divinity could create the like any moment it pleases You; why do You need, then, pour out Your soul unto death?" Such arguments would Satan use; the hellish craft of one who had then been thousands of years tempting men would know how to invent all manner of mischief. He would pour the hottest coals of hell upon the Savior. It was in struggling with this temptation, among others, that, being in an agony, our Savior prayed more earnestly.

Scripture implies that our Lord was assailed by *the fear that His strength would not be sufficient.* (See 2 Corinthians 12:9.) He was heard in that He feared. How, then, was He heard? An angel was sent unto Him, strengthening Him. His fear, then, was probably produced by a sense of weakness. I imagine that the foul fiend would whisper in His ear, "You! You endure to be smitten of God and abhorred of men! Reproach has broken Your heart already; how will You bear to be publicly put to shame and driven without the city as an unclean thing? How will You bear to see Your weeping kinsfolk and Your brokenhearted mother standing at the foot of Your cross? Your tender and sensitive spirit will quail under it. As for Your body, it is already emaciated; Your long fastings have brought You very low; You will become a prey to death long before Your work is done. You will surely fail. God has forsaken You. Now will they persecute and take You; they will give up Your soul to the lion, and Your darling to the power of the dog." Then would he picture all the sufferings of crucifixion, and say, "Can Your heart endure, or can Your hands be strong, in the day when the Lord shall deal with You?" The temptation of Satan was not directed against the Godhead but the manhood of Christ, and therefore the fiend would probably dwell upon the feebleness of man. "Did you not say Yourself, '*I am a worm, and no man; a reproach of men, and despised of the people*'" (Psalm 22:6)? How will You bear it when the wrath-clouds of God gather about You? The tempest will surely shipwreck all Your hopes. It cannot be You cannot drink of this cup, nor be baptized with this baptism." (See Mark 10:38.) In this manner, we think, was our Master tried. But see He yields not to it. Being in an agony, which word means in a wrest ring, He struggles with the tempter like Jacob with the angel. "Nay," He says, "I will not be subdued by taunts of My weakness. I am strong in the strength of My Godhead; I will overcome you yet." The temptation was so awful that, in order to master it, His mental depression caused Him to sweat *as it were great drops of blood falling down to the ground*" (Luke 22:44).

Possibly, also, the temptation may have arisen from a suggestion *that He was utterly forsaken.* There may be sterner trials than this, but surely this is *one* of the worst—to be utterly forsaken.

"See?" said Satan, as he hissed it out between his teeth. "See, You have a friend nowhere! Look up to heaven. Your Father has shut up the bowels of His compassion against You. Not an angel in Your Father's courts will stretch out his hand to help You. Look over there—not one of those spirits who honored Your birth will interfere to protect Your life. All heaven is false to You; You are left alone. And as for earth, do not all men thirst for Your blood? Will not the Jew be gratified to see Your flesh torn with nails, and will not the Roman gloat himself when You, the King of the Jews, are fastened to the cross? You have no friend among the nations; the high and mighty scoff at You, and the poor thrust out their tongues in derision. You had nowhere to lay Your head when You were in Your best estate; You have no place now where shelter will be given to You. See the companions with whom You have taken sweet counsel—what are they worth? Son of Mary, see there Your brother James, see there Your loved disciple John, and Your bold apostle Peter—they sleep, they sleep; and yonder eight, how the cowards sleep when You are in Your sufferings! And where are the four hundred others? They have forgotten You; they will be at their farms and their merchandise by morning. Lo! You have no friend left in heaven or earth. All hell is against You. I have stirred up my infernal den. I have sent my missives throughout all regions summoning every prince of darkness to set upon You this night, and we will spare no arrows; we will use all our infernal might to overwhelm Thee. And what will You do, You solitary one?" It may be that this was the temptation; I think it was, because the appearance of an angel unto Him strengthening Him removed that fear. (See Luke 22:43.) He was heard in that He feared; He was no more alone, but heaven was with Him. It may be that this is the reason of His coming three times to His disciples—as Hart puts it—

> Backwards and forwards thrice He ran
> As if He sought some help from man.

He would see for Himself whether it was really true that all men had forsaken Him—He found them all asleep—but perhaps He gained some faint comfort from the thought that they were sleeping not from treachery but from sorrow; the spirit indeed was willing, but the flesh was weak.

We think Satan also assaulted our Lord with a bitter taunt indeed. You know in what guise the tempter can dress it, and how bitterly sarcastic he can make the insinuation—"Ah! You will not be able to achieve the redemption of Your people. Your grand benevolence will prove a mockery, and Your beloved ones will perish. You shall not prevail to save them from my grasp. Your scattered sheep shall surely be my prey. Son of David, I am a match for You; You cannot deliver out of my hand. Many of Your chosen have entered heaven on the strength of Your atonement, but I will drag them there, and quench the stars of glory; I will thin the courts of heaven of the choristers of God, for You will not fulfill Your suretyship; You cannot do it. You are not able to bring up all these great people; they will perish yet. See, are not the sheep scattered now that the Shepherd is smitten? They will all forget You. You will never see of the travail of Your soul. Your desired end will never be reached. You will be forever the man that began to build but was not able to finish."

Perhaps this is more truly the reason why Christ went three times to look at His disciples. You have seen a mother; she is very faint, weary with a heavy sickness, but she labors under a sore dread that her child will die. She has started from her couch, upon which disease had thrown her, to snatch a moment's rest. She gazes anxiously upon her child. She marks the faintest sign of recovery. But she is sore sick herself and cannot remain more than an instant from her own bed. She cannot sleep; she tosses painfully, for her thoughts wander; she rises to gaze again—"How are you, my child, how are you? Are those palpitations of your heart less violent? Is your pulse more gentle?" But, alas! She is faint, and she must go to her bed again, yet she can get no rest. She will return repeatedly to watch the loved one. So, it seems to me, Christ looked upon Peter, and James, and John, as much as to say, "No, they are not all lost yet; there are three left," and, looking upon them as the type of all the church, He seemed to say, "No, no; I will overcome; I will get the mastery; I will struggle even unto blood; I will pay the ransom-price and deliver My darlings from their foe."

It seems to me that these were His temptations. If you can form a fuller idea of what they were than this, then right happy shall I be. With this one lesson I leave the point: *"Pray, that you enter not into temptation"* (Matthew 26:41). This is Christ's own expression, His own deduction from His trial. You have all read, dear friends, John Bunyan's picture of Christian fighting with Apollyon. That master-painter has sketched it to the very life. He says, though "this sore combat lasted for above half a day, even till Christian was almost quite spent, I never saw him all the while give so much as one pleasant look, till he perceived he had wounded Apollyon with his two-edged sword; then indeed, he did smile and look upward! But it was the dreadfullest sight I ever saw."[1] That is the meaning of that prayer, *"Lead us not into temptation"* (Matthew 6:13). Oh, you that go recklessly where you are tempted, you that pray for afflictions—and I have known some silly enough to do that—you that put yourselves where you tempt the devil to tempt you, take heed from the Master's own example. He sweats great drops of blood when He is tempted. Oh! Pray to God to spare you such trials. Pray this morning and every day, "Lead me not into temptation."

III. THE BLOODY SWEAT

We read that *"His sweat was as it were great drops of blood"* (Luke 22:44). Thus a few writers have supposed that the sweat was not actually blood but had the appearance of it. That interpretation, however, has been rejected by most commentators, from Augustine downward, and it is generally held that the words *"as it were"* do not only set forth *likeness* to blood but signify that it was actually and literally blood. We find the same idiom used in this text: *"We beheld His glory, the glory as of the only-begotten of the Father"* (John 1:14). Now, clearly, this does not mean that Christ was like the only begotten of the Father, since He is really so. So, generally, this expression of Holy Scripture sets forth not a mere likeness to a thing but the very thing itself. We believe, then, that Christ did really sweat blood. This phenomenon, though somewhat unusual, has been witnessed in other persons. There are

---

1 John Bunyan, *The Pilgrim's Progress* (New Kensington, PA: Whitaker House, 2017), 65–66.

several cases on record, some in the old medicine books of Galen, and others of more recent date, of persons who, after long weakness, under fear of death, have sweat blood. But this case is altogether one by itself for several reasons. If you will notice, He not only sweat blood, but it was in great drops; the blood coagulated and formed large masses. I cannot better express what is meant than by the word "gouts"—big, heavy drops. This has not been seen in any case. Some slight effusions of blood have been known in cases of persons who were previously enfeebled, but great drops never. When it is said *"falling to the ground"* it shows their copiousness, so that they not only stood upon the surface and were sucked up by His garments till He became like the red heifer which was slaughtered on that very spot, but the drops fell to the ground. Here He stands unrivalled. He was a man in good health, only about thirty years of age, and was laboring under no fear of death; but the mental pressure arising from His struggle with temptation, and the straining of all His strength in order to baffle the temptation of Satan, so forced His frame to an unnatural excitement, that His pores sent forth great drops of blood which fell down to the ground. This proves how tremendous must have been the weight of sin when it was able so to crush the Savior that He distilled drops of blood! This proves too, my brethren, the mighty power of His love. It is a very pretty observation of old Isaac Ambrose that the gum which exudes from the tree without cutting is always the best. This precious camphire-tree yielded most sweet spices when it was wounded under the knotty whips and when it was pierced by the nails on the cross; but, see, it gives forth its best spice when there is no whip, no nail, no wound. This sets forth the voluntariness of Christ's sufferings, since without a lance the blood flowed freely. No need to put on the leech or apply the knife; it flows spontaneously. No need for the rulers to cry, "Spring up, O well"; of itself it flows in crimson torrents. Dearly beloved friends, if men suffer some frightful pain of mind—I am not acquainted with the medical matter—apparently the blood rushes to the heart. The cheeks are pale; a fainting fit comes on; the blood has gone inward, as if to nourish the inner man while passing through its trial. But see our Savior in His agony; He is so utterly oblivious of self, that instead of His agony driving His blood to the heart to nourish Himself, it drives it outward to bedew the earth. The agony of Christ, inasmuch as it pours Him out upon the ground, pictures the fullness of the offering which He made for men.

Do you not perceive, my brethren, how intense must have been the wrestlings through which He passed, and will you not hear its voice *to you? "You have not yet resisted to blood, striving against sin"* (Hebrews 12:4). It has been the lot of some of us to have sore temptations—else we did not know how to teach others—so sore that in wrestling against them the cold, clammy sweat has stood upon our brow. The place will never be forgotten by me—a lonely spot where, musing upon my God, an awful rush of blasphemy went over my soul, till I would have preferred death to the trial; and I fell on my knees there and then, for the agony was awful, while my hand was at my mouth to keep the blasphemies from being spoken. Once let Satan be permitted really to try you with a temptation to blasphemy, and you will never forget it, though you live till your hairs are blanched; or let him attack you with some lust, and though you hate and loathe the very thought of it, and would lose your right arm sooner than indulge in it, yet it will come, and hunt, and persecute, and torment you. Wrestle against it even unto sweat, my brethren, yea, even unto blood. None of you should say, "I could not help it; I was tempted." Resist till you sweat blood rather than sin. Do not say, "I was so pressed with it, and it so suited my natural temperament, that I could not help falling into it." Look at the great Apostle and High Priest of your profession and sweat even to blood rather than yield to the great tempter of your souls. Pray that you enter not into temptation, so that when you enter into it, you may with confidence say, "Lord,

I did not seek this, therefore help me through with it, for Your name's sake."

IV. THE SAVIOR'S PRAYER

Dear friends, when we are tempted and desire to overcome, the best weapon is prayer. When you cannot use the sword and the shield, take to yourself the famous weapon of all-prayer. That is what your Savior did. Let us notice His prayer.

IT WAS LONELY PRAYER

He withdrew even from His three best friends about a stone's cast. Believer, especially in temptation, be much in solitary prayer. As private prayer is the key to open heaven, so is it the key to shut the gates of hell. As it is a shield to prevent, so is it the sword with which to fight against temptation. Family prayer, social prayer, prayer in the church will not suffice. These are very precious, but the best beaten spice will smoke in your censer in your private devotions, where no ear hears but God's. Betake yourselves to solitude if you would overcome.

IT WAS HUMBLE PRAYER

Luke says he knelt, but another evangelist says he fell on his face. What! Does the King fall on His face? Where, then, must be your place, you humble servant of the great Master? Doth the Prince fall flat to the ground? Where, then, will you lie? What dust and ashes shall cover your head? What sackcloth shall gird your loins? Humility gives us a good foothold in prayer. There is no hope of any real prevalence with God, who casts down the proud, unless we abase ourselves that He may exalt us in due time. (See 1 Peter 5:6.)

IT WAS FILIAL PRAYER

Matthew describes Him as saying, *"O My Father"* (Matthew 26:39); Mark puts it, *"Abba, Father"* (Mark 14:36). You will find this always a stronghold in the day of trial—to plead your adoption. Thus that prayer in which it is written, *"Lead us not into temptation, but deliver us from evil"* (Matthew 6:13) begins with *"Our Father which is in heaven"* (Matthew 6:9). Plead as a child. You have no rights as a subject; you have forfeited them by your treason, but nothing can forfeit a child's right to a father's protection. Be not then ashamed to say, "My Father, hear my cry."

IT WAS PERSEVERING PRAYER

He prayed three times, using the same words. Be not content until you prevail. Be as the importunate widow, whose continual coming earned what her first supplication could not win. (See Luke 18:1–8.) Continue in prayer and watch in the same with thanksgiving.

IT WAS EARNEST PRAYER

"He prayed more earnestly" (Luke 22:44). What groans were those which were uttered by Christ! What tears, which welled up from the deep fountains of His nature! Make earnest supplication if you would prevail against the adversary.

IT WAS THE PRAYER OF RESIGNATION

"Nevertheless not as I will, but as You will" (Matthew 26:39). Yield, and God yields. Let it be as God wills, and God will will it that it shall be for the best. Be perfectly content to leave the result of your prayer in the hands of Him who knows when to give, and how to give, and what to give, and what to withhold. So pleading, earnestly, importunately, yet mingling with it humility and resignation, you shall yet prevail.

Dear friends, we must conclude; turn to the last point, with this as a practical lesson: rise and pray. When the disciples were lying down, they slept; sitting was the posture that was congenial to sleep. Rise; shake yourselves; stand up in the name of God; rise and pray. And if you are in temptation, be you, more than ever you were in your life before, instant, passionate, importunate with God, that He would deliver you in the day of your conflict.

V. THE SAVIOR'S PREVALENCE

The cloud has passed away. Christ has knelt, and the prayer is over. "But," says one, "did Christ prevail in prayer?" Beloved, could we have any hope that He would prevail in heaven if He had not prevailed on earth? Should we not have had a suspicion that if His strong crying and tears had not been heard *then*, He would fail *now*? His prayers did speed, and therefore He is a good intercessor for us. "How was He heard?" The answer shall be given very briefly indeed. He was heard, I think, in three respects.

JESUS'S MIND WAS SUDDENLY RENDERED CALM

What a difference there is between "*My soul is exceeding sorrowful*" (Matthew 26:38)—His hurrying to and fro, His repetition of the prayer three times, the singular agitation that was upon Him—what a contrast between all these and His going forth to meet the traitor with this statement: "*Betray you the Son of Man with a kiss?*" (Luke 22:48). Like a troubled sea before, and now as calm as when He Himself said, "*Peace, be still*" (Mark 4:39), and the waves were quiet. You cannot know a profounder peace than that which reigned in the Savior when before Pilate He answered him not a word. (See Matthew 27:14.) He is calm to the last, as calm as though it were His day of triumph rather than His day of trouble. Now I think this was vouchsafed to Him in answer to His prayer. He had sufferings perhaps more intense, but His mind was now quieted so as to meet them with greater deliberation. Like some men who, when they first hear the firing of the shots in a battle, are all trepidation, but as the fight grows hotter and they are in greater danger, they are cool and collected—they are wounded, they are bleeding, they are dying, yet are they quiet as a summer's eve; the first young flush of trouble is gone, and they can meet the foe with peace—so the Father heard the Savior's cry, and breathed such a profound peace into His soul, that it was like a river, and His righteousness like the waves of the sea. (See Isaiah 48:18.)

WE BELIEVE THAT JESUS WAS ANSWERED BY GOD STRENGTHENING HIM THROUGH AN ANGEL

How that was done we do not know. Probably it was by what the angel said, and equally likely is it that it was by what he did. The angel may have whispered the promises; pictured before His mind's eye the glory of His success; sketched His resurrection; portrayed the scene when His angels would bring His chariots from on high to bear Him to His throne; revived before Him the recollection of the time of His advent, the prospect when He should reign from sea to sea, and from the river even to the ends of the earth; and so have made Him strong. Or, perhaps, by some unknown method, God sent such power to our Christ, who had been like Samson with his locks shorn (see Judges 16:19), that He suddenly received all the might and majestic energy that were needed for the terrific struggle. Then He walked out of the garden no more a worm and no man, but made strong with an invisible might that made Him a match for all the armies that were round about Him. A troop had overcome Him, like Gad of old, but He overcame at last. (See Genesis 49:19.) Now He can dash through a troop; now He can leap over a wall. (See Psalm 18:29.) God has sent by His angel force from on high and made the man Christ strong for battle and for victory.

GOD GRANTED JESUS A REAL VICTORY OVER SATAN

I do not know whether what Adam Clarke supposes is correct, that in the garden Christ did pay more of the price than He did even on the cross; but I am quite convinced that they are very foolish who get to such refinement that they think the atonement was made on the cross and nowhere else at all. We believe that it was made in the garden as well as on the cross; and it strikes me that in the garden one part of Christ's work was finished, wholly finished, and that was His conflict with Satan. I conceive that Christ had now rather to bear the absence of His Father's presence and the revilings of the people and the sons of men than the temptations of the devil. I do think that these were over when He rose from His knees in prayer, when He lifted Himself from the ground where He marked His visage in the clay in drops of blood. The temptation of Satan was then over, and He might have said, concerning that part of the work, "It is finished; broken is the dragon's head; I have overcome him."

Perhaps in those few hours that Christ spent in the garden the whole energy of the agents of iniquity was concentrated and dissipated. Perhaps in that one conflict all that craft could invent, all that malice could devise, all that infernal practice could suggest, was tried on Christ, the devil having his chain loosened for that purpose, having Christ given up to him, as Job was (see Job 1–2), that he might touch Him in His bones and in His flesh, yea, touch Him in His heart and His soul, and vex Him in His spirit. It may be that every devil in hell and every fiend of the pit was summoned, each to vent his own spite and to pour their united energy and malice upon the head of Christ. And there He stood, and He could have said as He stood up to meet the next adversary—a devil in the form of man, Judas—"I come this day from Bozrah, with garments dyed red from Edom; I have trampled on My enemies and overcome them once for all; now go I to bear man's sin and My Father's wrath, and to finish the work which He has given Me to do." (See Isaiah 63:1–6.) If this be so, Christ was then heard in that He feared; He feared the temptation of Satan, and He was delivered from it; He feared His own weakness, and He was strengthened; He feared His own trepidation of mind, and He was made calm.

What shall we say, then, in conclusion, but this lesson? Does it not say, "*Whatsoever you shall ask in prayer, believing, you shall receive*" (Matthew 21:22)? Then if your temptations reach the most tremendous height and force, still lay hold of God in prayer, and you shall prevail. Convinced sinner! That is a comfort for you. Troubled saint! That is a joy for you. To one and all of us is this lesson of this morning: *"Pray, that you enter not into temptation"* (Matthew 26:41). If in temptation, let us ask that Christ may pray for us that our faith fail not, and when we have passed through the trouble, let us try to strengthen our brethren, even as Christ has strengthened us this day.

2

THE PRECIOUS BLOOD OF CHRIST

"The precious blood of Christ."
—1 Peter 1:19

Blood has from the beginning been regarded by God as a most precious thing. He has hedged about this fountain of vitality with the most solemn sanctions. The Lord thus commanded Noah and his descendants, *"Flesh with the life thereof, which is the blood thereof, shall you not eat"* (Genesis 9:4). Man had every moving thing that lives given him for meat, but he was by no means to eat the blood with the flesh. Things strangled were to be considered unfit for food, since God would not have man become too familiar with blood by eating or drinking it in any shape or form. Even the blood of bulls and goats thus had a sacredness put upon it by God's decrees.

As for the blood of man, you remember how God's threats ran: *"And surely your blood of your lives will I require; at the hand of every beast will I require it, and at the hand of man; at the hand of every man's brother will I require the life of man. Whoso sheds man's blood, by man shall his blood be shed: for in the image of God made He man"* (Genesis 9:5–6). It is true that the first murderer had not his blood shed by man, but then the crime was new, and the penalty had not then been settled and proclaimed. Therefore, the case was clearly exceptional and one by itself. And, moreover, Cain's doom was probably far more terrible than if he had been slain upon the spot—he was permitted to fill up his measure of wickedness, to be a wanderer and a vagabond upon the face of the earth—and then to enter into the dreadful heritage of wrath, which his life of sin had doubtless greatly increased. (See Genesis 4.)

Under the theocratic dispensation, in which God was the King and governed Israel, murder was always punished in the most exemplary manner; there was never any toleration or excuse for it. Eye for eye, tooth for tooth, life for life was the stern, inexorable law. (See Exodus 21:23–25.) It is expressly written, "*You shall take no satisfaction for the life of a murderer, which is guilty of death: but he shall surely be put to death*" (Numbers 35:31). Even in cases where life was taken in chance medley or misadventure, the matter was not overlooked. The slayer fled at once to a city of refuge where, after having his case properly tried, he was allowed to reside. But there was no safety for him elsewhere until the death of the high priest. (See Numbers 35:32.)

The general law in all cases was, "*So you shall not pollute the land wherein you are: for blood it defiles the land: and the land cannot be cleansed of the blood that is shed therein, but by the blood of him that shed it. Defile not therefore the land which you shall inhabit, wherein I dwell: for I the* LORD *dwell among the children of Israel*" (Numbers 35:33–34). Strange it is that that very thing which defiles should turn out to be that which alone can cleanse! It is clear, then, that blood was ever precious in God's sight, and He would have it so in ours.

He first forbids the blood of beasts as food of man, then avenges the blood of man shed in anger and, furthermore, takes care that even accidents shall not pour it out unheeded. Nor is this all. We hear within us the echo of that law. We feel that God has truly made blood a sacred thing. Though some can, through use and habit, read the story of war with patience, if not with pleasure—though the sound of the trumpet and the drum and the tramp of soldiery will stir our heart and make us, for the moment, sympathize with the martial spirit—yet, if we could see war as it really is, if we could only walk but halfway across a battlefield or see but one wounded man, a cold shiver would shoot through the very marrow of our bones, and we should have experimental proof that blood is, indeed, a sacred thing.

The other night, when I listened to one who professed to have come from battlefields of the American war, I felt a faintness and a clammy sweat steal over me as he shocked and horrified us with the details of mutilated bodies and spoke of standing up to the tops of his boots in pools of human gore. The shudder which ran through us all was a sure confirmation of the sanctity with which God has forever guarded the symbol and nutriment of life. We cannot even contemplate the probability of the shedding of blood without fear and trembling.

And comforts which entail high risks in their production or procuring will lose all sweetness to men of humane dispositions. Who does not sympathize with David in his action with regard to the water procured by his three mighty men? The three heroes broke through the hosts of the Philistines to bring David water from the well of Bethlehem. But as soon as he received that water, though very thirsty and much longing for it, yet he felt he could not touch it because these men had run such dreadful risks in breaking thrice through the Philistine hosts to bring it to him! He, therefore, took the water and poured it out before the Lord, as if it was not meet that men should run risk of life for any but God who gave life. (See 1 Chronicles 11:18–19.)

His words were very touching: *"My God forbid it me, that I should do this thing: shall I drink the blood of these men that have put their lives in jeopardy? For with the jeopardy or their lives they brought it"* (1 Chronicles 11:19). I wonder at the cruelty of the great crowds who delight to see men and women running such fearful risks of life in rope-dancing. How is it that they can feed their morbid curiosity on such dreadful food and greet the man who is foolish enough to run such hazards with acclamations because of his fool-hardiness? How much more Christlike the regret of David that he should have led any man to risk his life for his comfort! How much more laudable was his belief that nothing short of the high-est benevolence to man or the highest devotion to God can justify such jeopardy of life!

Further permit me to observe that the seal of the sanctity of blood is usually set upon the conscience even of the most depraved of men—not merely upon gentle souls and sanctified spirits but even upon the most hardened. You will notice that men, bad as they are, shrink from the disgrace of taking blood money. Even those high priests who could sit down and gloat their eyes with the sufferings of the Savior would not receive the price of blood into the treasury. (See Matthew 27:6.) And even Judas, that son of perdition, who could contemplate without horror the treachery by which he betrayed his Master—when he had the thirty pieces of silver in his palm, he found the money too hot to hold! He threw it down in the temple, for he could not bear or abide the sight of "the price of blood." (See Matthew 27:5.) This is another proof that even when virtue has become extinct and vice reigns, yet God has put the broad arrow of His own sovereignty so manifestly upon the very thought of blood that even these worst of spirits are com-pelled to shrink from tampering with it.

Now, if in ordinary cases the shedding of life is thus precious, can you guess how fully God utters His heart's meaning when He says, *"Precious in the sight of the LORD is the death of His saints"* (Psalm 116:15)? If the death of a rebel is precious, what must be the death of a child? If He will not contemplate the shedding of the blood of His own enemies and of them that curse Him without proclaiming vengeance, what do you think He feels concerning His own elect, of whom He says, *"Precious shall their blood be in his sight"* (Psalm 72:14)? Will He not avenge them, though He bears long with them?

Shall the cup which the harlot of Rome filled with the blood of the saints long remain unavenged? Shall not the martyrs from Piedmont and the Alps and from our Smithfield and from the hills of covenanting Scotland yet obtain from God the vengeance due for all that they suffered and all the blood which they poured forth in the defense of His cause? I have taken you up, you see, from the beast to man—from man to God's chosen men—the martyrs. I have another step to indicate to you, and it is a far larger one—it is to the blood of *Jesus Christ*.

Here powers of speech would fail to convey to you an idea of the preciousness! Behold here, a person innocent—without taint within or flaw without! A person meritorious who magnified the Law and made it honorable—a person who served both God and man even unto death. No, here you have a divine person—so divine that in the Acts of the Apostles Paul calls His blood the "blood of God." (See Acts 20:28.) Place innocence and merit and dignity and position and Godhead itself in the scale and then conceive what must be the inestimable value of the blood which Jesus Christ poured forth!

Angels must have seen that matchless blood-shedding with wonder and amazement, and even God Himself saw what never before was seen in creation or in providence—He saw Himself more gloriously displayed than the whole universe beside.

Let us come nearer to the text and try to show forth the preciousness of the blood of Christ. We shall confine ourselves to an enumeration of some of the many properties possessed by this precious blood.

I felt, as I was studying, that I should have so many divisions this morning that some of you would compare my sermon to the bones in Ezekiel's vision—they were very many and they were very dry (see Ezekiel 37:1–14)—but I am in hopes that God's Holy Spirit may so descend upon the bones in my sermon—which would be but dry of themselves—that, they being quickened and full of life, you may admire the exceeding great army of God's thoughts of loving-kindness toward His people in the sacrifice of His own dear Son.

The precious blood of Christ is useful to God's people in a thousand ways—we intend to speak of twelve of them. After all, the real preciousness of a thing in the time of pinch and trial must depend upon its usefulness. A bag of pearls would be to us, this morning, far more precious than a bag of bread. But you have all heard the story of the man in the desert who stumbled, when near to death, upon a bag. He opened it, hoping that it might be the wallet of some passerby, and he found in it nothing but pearls! If they had been crusts of bread, how much more precious would they have been! I say, in the hour of necessity and peril, the use of a thing really constitutes the preciousness of it. This may not be according to political economy, but it is according to common sense.

I. THE PRECIOUS BLOOD OF CHRIST HAS A REDEEMING POWER

It redeems from the law. We were all under the law which says, "*This do, and you shall live*" (Luke 10:28). We were slaves to it—Christ has paid the ransom price, and the law is no longer our tyrant master. We are entirely free from it. The law had a dreadful curse—it threatened that whoever should violate one of its precepts should die: "*Christ has redeemed us from the curse of the law, being made a curse for us*" (Galatians 3:13).

By the fear of this curse the law inflicted a continual dread on those who were under it. They knew they had disobeyed it, and they were all their lifetime subject to bondage, fearful lest death and destruction should come upon them at any moment. But we are not under the law; we are under grace (see Romans 6:14), and, consequently, we *"have not received the spirit of bondage again to fear, but we have received the Spirit of adoption, whereby we cry, Abba, Father"* (Romans 8:15).

We are not afraid of the law now—its worst thunders cannot affect us, for they are not hurled at us! Its most tremendous lightning cannot touch us, for we are sheltered beneath the cross of Christ, where the thunder loses its terror and the lightning its fury. We read the law of God with pleasure now! We look upon it as in the ark covered with the mercy seat and not thundering in tempests from Sinai's fiery brow. Happy is that person who knows their full redemption from the law, its curse, its penalty, its present dread!

My brethren, the life of a Jew, happy as it was compared with that of a heathen, was perfect drudgery compared to yours and mine! He was hedged in with a thousand commands and prohibitions. His forms and ceremonies were abundant, their details minutely arranged. He was always in danger of making himself unclean. If he sat upon a bed or upon a stool he might be defiled. If he drank out of an earthen pitcher or even touched the wall of a house—a leprous man might have put his hand there before him, and he would thus become defiled. A thousand sins of ignorance were like so many hidden pits in his way. He must be perpetually in fear lest he should be cut off from the people of God.

When he had done his best any one day, he knew he had not finished—no Jew could ever talk of a finished work. The bullock was offered, but he must bring another. The lamb was offered this morning, but another must be offered this evening, another tomorrow, and another the next day. The Passover is celebrated with holy rites—it must be kept in the same manner next year. The high priest has gone within the veil once but must go there again. The thing is never finished—it is always beginning. He never comes any nearer to the end. The law could not make the comer *"thereunto perfect"* (Hebrews 10:1).

But see our position—we are redeemed from this! Our law is fulfilled, for Christ is the end of the law for righteousness! Our Passover is slain, for Jesus died! Our righteousness is finished, for we are complete in Him! Our victim is slain, our Priest has gone within the veil, the blood is sprinkled! We are clean, and clean beyond any fear of defilement, for *"He has perfected for ever them that are sanctified"* (Hebrews 10:14). Value this precious blood, my beloved, because thus it has redeemed you from the bondage which the law imposed upon its votaries.

II. THE VALUE OF THE BLOOD LIES MUCH IN ITS ATONING EFFICACY

We are told in Leviticus that *"it is the blood that makes an atonement for the soul"* (Leviticus 17:11). God never forgave sin apart from blood under the law. This stood as a constant text: *"Without shedding of blood is no remission"* (Hebrews 9:22). Meal and honey, sweet spices and incense would not avail without shedding of blood. There was no remission promised to future diligence or deep repentance—without shedding of blood pardon never came. The blood, and the blood alone, put away sin and permitted a man to come to God's courts to worship—because it made him one with God.

The blood is the great at-one-ment. There is no hope of pardon for the sin of any man except through its punishment being fully endured. God must punish sin. It is not an arbitrary arrangement that sin shall be punished, but it is a part of the very constitution of moral government that sin must be punished. Never did God swerve from that, and never will He. "He will by no means clear the guilty." (See Exodus 34:7.)

Christ, therefore, came and was punished in the place of all His people. Ten thousand times ten thousand are the souls for whom Jesus shed His blood. He, for the sins of all the elect, has made a complete atonement. For every man born of Adam who has believed or shall believe on Him, or who is taken to glory before being capable of believing, Christ has made a complete atonement. And there is no other plan by which sinners can be made at one with God, except by Jesus's precious blood.

I may make sacrifices. I may mortify my body. I may be baptized. I may receive sacraments. I may pray until my knees grow hard with kneeling. I may read devout words until I know them by heart. I may celebrate masses. I may worship in one language or in fifty languages—but I can never be at one with God except by blood—and that blood, *"the precious blood of Christ"* (1 Peter 1:19).

My dear friends, many of you have felt the power of Christ's redeeming blood! You are not under the law now but under grace. You have also felt the power of the atoning blood; you know that you are reconciled unto God by the death of His Son. You feel that He is no angry God to you, that He loves you with a love unchangeable. But this is not the case with you all. O that it were! I do pray that you may know, this very day, the atoning power of the blood of Jesus! Creature, would you not be at one with your Creator? Puny man, would you not have almighty God to be your Friend? You cannot be at one with God except through the at-one-ment. God has set forth Christ to be a propitiation for our sins. Oh, take the propitiation through faith in His blood and be at one with God!

III. THE PRECIOUS BLOOD OF JESUS CHRIST HAS A CLEANSING POWER

John tells us in his first epistle, first chapter, seventh verse, *"The blood of Jesus Christ His Son cleanses us from all sin"* (1 John 1:7). Sin has a directly defiling effect upon the sinner, from which comes the need of cleansing. Suppose that God, the Holy One, were perfectly willing to be at one with an unholy sinner, which is supposing a case that cannot be. Yet even should the pure eyes of the Most High wink at sin, still, as long as we are unclean, we never could feel in our own hearts anything like joy and rest and peace.

Sin is a plague to the man who has it, as well as a hateful thing to the God who abhors it. I must be made clean. I must have my iniquities washed away or I never can be happy. The first mercy that is sung of in the one hundred and third Psalm is that God "*forgives all your iniquities*" (Psalm 103:3). Now we know it is by the precious blood that sin is cleansed. Murder, adultery, theft—whatever the sin may be—there is power in the veins of Christ to take it away at once and forever! No matter how many, nor how deeply seated, our offenses may be, the blood cries, "*Though your sins be as scarlet, they shall be as white as snow; though they be red like crimson, they shall be as wool*" (Isaiah 1:18).

It is the song of heaven—"We have washed our robes and made them white in the blood of the Lamb." (See Revelation 7:14.) This is the experience of earth, for none was ever cleansed except in this fountain opened for the house of David for sin and for uncleanness. You have heard this so often that perhaps if an angel told it to you, you would not take much interest in it—unless you have known experimentally the horror of uncleanness and the blessedness of being made clean. Beloved, it is a thought which ought to make our hearts leap within us, that through Jesus's blood there is not a spot left upon any believer, not a wrinkle nor any such thing—oh, precious blood, removing the Hell-stains of abundant iniquity and permitting me to stand accepted in the Beloved, notwithstanding all the many ways in which I have rebelled against my God!

IV. A PROPERTY OF THE BLOOD OF CHRIST IS ITS PRESERVING POWER

You will rightly comprehend this when you remember that dreadful night of Egypt when the destroying angel was abroad to slay God's enemies. A bitter cry went up from house to house as the firstborn of all Egypt—from Pharaoh on the throne to the firstborn of the woman behind the mill and the slave in the dungeon—all fell dead in a moment! The angel sped with noiseless wings through every street of Egypt's many cities. (See Exodus 12:29–30.)

But there were some houses which he could not enter—he sheathed his sword and breathed no malediction there. What was it which preserved the houses? The inhabitants were not better than others. Their habitations were not more elegantly built. There was nothing except the bloodstain on the lintel and on the two side posts, and it is written: *"When I see the blood, I will pass over you"* (Exodus 12:13). There was nothing whatever which gained the Passover for Israel but the sprinkling of blood!

The father of the house had taken a lamb and killed it—had caught the blood in a basin. And while the lamb was roasted so that it might be eaten by every inhabitant of the house, he took a bunch of hyssop, stirred the basin of blood, went outside with his children, and began to strike the posts and to strike the door. And as soon as this was done, they were all safe, all safe—no angel could touch them; the fiends of hell themselves could not venture there.

Beloved, see, we are preserved in Christ Jesus! Did not God see the blood before you and I saw it, and was not that the reason why He spared our forfeited lives when, like barren fig trees, we brought forth no fruit for Him? When we saw the blood, let us remember it was not our seeing it which really saved us—one sight of it gave us peace, but it was God's seeing it that saved us. *"When I see the blood, I will pass over you"* (Exodus 12:13).

And today, if my eye of faith is dim and I see the precious blood so as to rejoice that I am washed but I can scarcely see it, yet God can see the blood; and as long as the undimmed eyes of Jehovah look upon the atoning sacrifice of the Lord Jesus, He cannot smite one soul that is covered with its scarlet mantle. Oh, how precious is this bloodred shield! My soul, cower yourself down under it when the darts of hell are flying! This is the chariot, the covering of purple—let the storm come and the deluge rise, let even the fiery hail descend beneath that crimson pavilion—my soul must rest secure, for what can touch me when I am covered with His precious blood?

The preserving power of that blood should make us feel how precious it is. Beloved, let me beg you to try to realize these points. You know I told you before I cannot say anything new upon the subject; neither can I embody these old thoughts in new words. I should only spoil them and be making a fool of myself by trying to make a display of myself and my own powers, instead of the precious blood. Let me ask you to get here, right under the shelter of the cross. Sit down, now, beneath the shadow of the cross and feel, "I am safe, I am safe, O you devils of hell, or you angels of God—I could challenge you all and say, 'Who shall separate me from the love of God in Christ Jesus (see Romans 8:35–39), or who shall lay anything to my charge, seeing that Christ has died for me?'"

When heaven is on a blaze, when the earth begins to shake, when the mountains rock, when God divides the righteous from the wicked—happy will they be who can find a shelter beneath the blood! But where will you be who have never trusted in its cleansing power? You will call to the rocks to hide you and to the mountains to cover you, but all in vain. God help you now, or even the blood will not help you then!

V. THE BLOOD OF CHRIST IS PRECIOUS BECAUSE OF ITS PLEADING PREVALENCE

The author of the epistle to the Hebrews that it *"speaks better things than that of Abel"* (Hebrews 12:24). Abel's blood pleaded and prevailed. Its cry was, "Vengeance!" and Cain was punished. (See Genesis 4:10–12.) Jesus's blood pleads and prevails. Its cry is, "Father, forgive them!" (see Luke 23:34) and sinners are forgiven through it.

When I cannot pray as I would, how sweet to remember that the blood prays! There is no voice in my tongue, but there is always a voice in the blood. If I cannot, when I bow before my God, get farther than to say, "God be merciful to me, a sinner," yet my Advocate before the throne is not dumb because I am, and His plea has not lost its power because my faith in it may happen to be diminished. The blood is always alike prevalent with God. The wounds of Jesus are so many mouths to plead with God for sinners—what if I say they are so many chains with which love is led captive and sovereign mercy bound to bless every favored child?

What if I say that the wounds of Jesus have become doors of divine grace through which divine love comes forth to the vilest of the vile and doors through which our wants go up to God and plead with Him that He would be pleased to supply them? Next time you cannot pray—next time you are crying and striving and groaning up in that upper room—praise the value of the precious blood which makes intercession before the eternal throne of God!

VI. THE BLOOD IS PRECIOUS BECAUSE OF ITS MELTING INFLUENCE ON THE HUMAN HEART

"They shall look upon Me whom they have pierced, and they shall mourn for Him, as one mourns for his only son, and shall

be in bitterness for Him, as one that is in bitterness for his firstborn." (Zechariah 12:10)

There is a great complaint among sinners, when they are a little awakened, that they feel their hearts so hard. The blood is a mighty melter. Alchemists of old sought after a universal solvent—the blood of Jesus is that. There is no nature so stubborn that a sight of the love of God in Christ Jesus cannot melt it if grace shall open the blind eye to see Christ. The stone in the human heart shall melt away when it is plunged into a bath of divine blood. Cannot you say, dear friends, that Toplady was right in his hymn—

> Law and terrors do but harden,
> All the while they work alone:
> But a sense of blood-bought pardon
> Soon dissolves a heart of stone?

Sinner, if God shall lead you to believe this morning in Christ to save you—if, then, you will trust your soul in His hands to have it saved—that hard heart of yours will melt at once! You would think differently of sin, my friends, if you knew that Christ smarted for it. Oh, if you knew that out of those dear, listless eyes there looked the loving heart of Jesus upon you, I know you would say, "I hate the sin that made Him mourn and fastened Him to the accursed tree."

I do not think that preaching the law generally softens men's hearts. Hitting men with a hard hammer may often drive the particles of a hard heart more closely together and make the iron yet more hard. But, oh, to preach Christ's love—His great love with which He loved us even when we were dead in sins, and to tell sinners that there is life in a look at the Crucified One—surely this will prove that Christ was exalted on high to give repentance and remission of sins! Come for repentance if you cannot come repenting! Come for a broken heart if you cannot come with a broken heart! Come to be melted if you are not melted. Come to be wounded if you are not wounded.

VII. THE PRECIOUS BLOOD OF JESUS CHRIST HAS A GRACIOUS POWER TO PACIFY

John Bunyan speaks of the law as coming to sweep a chamber like a maid with a broom. And when she began to sweep, there was a great dust which almost choked people and got into their eyes. But then came the gospel with its drops of water and laid the dust, and then the broom might be used far better.

Now it sometimes happens that the law of God makes such a dust in the sinner's soul that nothing but the precious blood of Jesus Christ can make that dust lie still. The sinner is so disquieted that nothing can ever give him any relief except to know that Jesus died for him. When I felt the burden of my sin, I do confess, all the preaching I ever heard never gave me one single atom of comfort. I was told to do this and to do that, and when I had done it all, I had not advanced one inch farther.

I thought I must feel something or pray a certain quantity. And when I had done that, the burden was quite as heavy. But the moment I saw that there was nothing whatever for me to do, that Jesus did it long, long ago—that all my sins were put on His back and that He suffered all I ought to have suffered—why then my heart had peace with God. Real peace by believing peace through the precious blood!

Two soldiers were on duty in the citadel of Gibraltar. One of them had obtained peace through the precious blood of Christ; the other was in very great distress of mind. It happened to be their turn to stand sentinel, both of them, the same night. And there are many long passages in the rock, which passages are adapted to convey sounds a very great distance. The soldier in distress of mind was ready to beat his breast for grief—he felt he had rebelled against God and could not find how he could be reconciled—when suddenly there came through the air what seemed to him to be a mysterious voice from heaven saying these words: "The precious blood of Christ."

In a moment he saw it all—it was that which reconciled us to God—and he rejoiced with joy unspeakable and full of glory! Now, did those words come directly from God? No. They did as far as the effect was concerned—they did come from the Holy Spirit. Who was it that had spoken those words? Curiously enough, the other sentinel at the far end of the passage was standing still and meditating when an officer came by, and it was his duty, of course, to give the word for the night, and so with soldierlike promptness he did give it—but not accurately, for instead of giving the proper word, he was so taken up by his meditations that he said to the officer, "The precious blood of Christ."

He corrected himself in a moment. But he had said it, and it had passed along the passage and reached the ear for which God meant it—and the man found peace and spent his life in the fear of God, being in after years the means of completing one of our excellent translations of the Word of God into the Hindu language. Who can tell, dear friends, how much peace you may give by only telling the story of our Savior! If I only had about a dozen words to speak, and knew I must die, I would say, *"This is a faithful saying, and worthy of all acceptation, that Christ Jesus came into the world to save sinners"* (1 Timothy 1:15). The doctrine of substitution is the pith and marrow of the gospel, and if you can hold that forth, you will prove the value of the precious blood by its peace-giving power.

VIII. THE PRECIOUS BLOOD OF CHRIST HAS SANCTIFYING INFLUENCE

Hebrews tells us that Christ sanctified the people by His own blood. (See Hebrews 9:14.) Certain it is that the same blood which justifies by taking away sin does, in its after-action, act upon the new nature and lead it onward to subdue sin and to follow out the commands of God. There is no motive for holiness so great as that which streams from the veins of Jesus. If you want to know why you should be obedient to God's will, my brethren, go and look upon Him who sweat, as it were, great drops of blood, and the love of Christ will constrain you, because you will thus judge, *"That if one died for all, then were all dead: And that He died for all, that they which live should not hereafter live to themselves, but to Him which died for them, and rose again"* (2 Corinthians 5:14–15).

IX. ANOTHER BLESSED PROPERTY OF THE BLOOD OF JESUS IS ITS POWER TO GIVE ENTRANCE

We are told that the high priest never went within the veil without blood. (See Hebrews 9:7.) And, surely, we can never get into God's heart, nor into the secret of the Lord, which is with them that fear Him, nor into any familiar communion with our great Father and Friend, except by the sprinkling of the precious blood of Jesus.

"We have access by faith into this grace wherein we stand" (Romans 5:2), but we never dare go a step toward God except as we are sprinkled with this precious blood. I am persuaded some of us do not come near to God because we forget the blood. If you try to have fellowship with God in your graces, your experiences, your believing—you will fail. But if you try to come near to God as you stand in Christ Jesus—you will have courage to come. And on the other hand, God will run to meet you when He sees you in the face of His Anointed. Oh, for power to get near to God! But there is no getting near to God except as we get near to the cross. Praise the blood, then, for its power of giving you nearness to God.

X. THE BLOOD OF JESUS CHRIST IS PRECIOUS FOR ITS CONFIRMING POWER

No covenant, we are told, was ever valid unless victims were slain, and blood sprinkled. (See Exodus 24:1–8). And it is the blood of Jesus which has ratified the new covenant and made its promises sure to all the seed. Therefore, it is called *"the blood of the everlasting covenant"* (Hebrews 13:20). The author of Hebrews changes the figure, and he says that a testament is not of force except the testator is dead. The blood is a proof that the Testator died, and now the law holds good to every inheritor because Jesus Christ has signed it with His own gore.

Beloved, let us rejoice that the promises are yes and amen (see 2 Corinthians 1:20), for no other reason than this—because Christ Jesus died and rose again. Had there been no bowing of the head upon the tree, no slumbering in the sepulcher, no rising from the tomb, then the promises had been uncertain, fickle things—not *"immutable things, wherein it was impossible for God to lie"* (Hebrews 6:18)—and consequently they could never have afforded strong consolation to those who have fled for refuge to Christ Jesus. See, then, the confirming nature of the blood of Jesus and count it very precious.

XI. THE PRECIOUS BLOOD OF CHRIS HAS INVIGORATING POWER

If you want to know the invigorating power of the precious blood of Christ, you must see it set forth as we often do when we cover the table with the white cloth and put the bread and wine on it. What do we mean by this ordinance? We mean by it that Christ suffered for us and that we, being already washed in His precious blood and so made clean, do come to the table to drink wine as an emblem of the way in which we live and feed upon His body and upon His blood.

He tells us, "*Except you eat the flesh of the Son of Man, and drink His blood, you have no life in you*" (John 6:53). We do therefore, after a spiritual sort, drink His blood, and He says, "*My blood is drink indeed*" (John 6:55). Superior drink! Transcendent drink! Strengthening drink—such drink as angels never taste, though they drink before the eternal throne. Oh, beloved, whenever your spirit faints, this wine shall comfort you! When your griefs are many, drink and forget your misery, and remember your sufferings no more!

When you are very weak and faint, take not a little of this for your soul's sake, but drink a full draught of the wine on the lees, well refined, which was set abroad by the soldier's spike and flowed from Christ's own heart! "*Drink, yea, drink abundantly, O beloved*" (Song of Solomon 5:1), says Christ to the spouse. And do not linger when He invites. You see, the blood has power without to cleanse, and then it has power within to strengthen. O precious blood, how many are your uses! May I prove them all!

XII. THE PRECIOUS BLOOD OF JESUS CHRIST HAS OVERCOMING POWER

It is written in the Revelation, "*They overcame him by the blood of the Lamb*" (Revelation 12:11). How could they do otherwise? He that fights with the precious blood of Jesus fights with a weapon that will cut through soul and spirit, joints, and marrow (see Hebrews 4:12)—a weapon that makes hell tremble and makes heaven subservient and earth obedient to the will of the men who can wield it!

The blood of Jesus! Sin dies at its presence, death ceases to be death—hell itself would be dried up if that blood could operate there. The blood of Jesus! Heaven's gates are opened! Bars of iron are pushed back. The blood of Jesus! My doubts and fears flee, my troubles and disasters disappear! The blood of Jesus! Shall I not go on conquering and to conquer so long as I can plead that?

In heaven this shall be the choice jewel which shall glitter upon the head of Jesus—that He gives to His people "Victory, victory, through the blood of the Lamb."

And now, is this blood to be had? Can it be got at? Yes, it is *free*, as well as full of virtue—free to every soul that believes. (See John 3:15–16). Whoever cares to come and trust in Jesus shall find the virtue of this blood in his case this very morning. Away from your own works! Turn those eyes of yours to the full atonement made to the utmost ransom paid! And if God enables you, poor soul, this morning to say, "I take that precious blood to be my only hope," you are saved, and you may sing with the rest of us:

> Now, freed from sin, I walk at large;
> The Savior's blood's my full discharge.
> At His dear feet my soul I'll lay,
> A sinner saved and homage pay.

3

MOURNING AT THE SIGHT
OF THE CRUCIFIED

"And all the people that came together to that sight,
beholding the things which were done,
smote their breasts, and returned."
—Luke 23:48

Many in that crowd came together to behold the crucifixion of Jesus, in a condition of the most furious malice. They had hounded the Savior as dogs pursue a stag and at last, all mad with rage, they hemmed Him in for death. Others, willing enough to spend an idle hour and to gaze upon a sensational spectacle, swelled the mob until a vast assembly congregated around the little hill upon which the three crosses were raised. There unanimously, whether of malice or of wantonness, they all joined in mockery of the Victim who hung upon the center cross. Some thrust out their tongues. Some wagged their heads. Others scoffed and jeered. Some taunted Him in words and others in signs, but all alike exulted over the defenseless Man who was given as a prey to their teeth.

Earth never beheld a scene in which so much unrestrained derision and expressive contempt were poured upon one man so unanimously and for so long a time. It must have been hideous to the last degree to have seen so many grinning faces and mocking eyes and to have heard so many cruel words and scornful shouts. The spectacle was too detestable to be long endured of heaven. Suddenly the sun, shocked at the scene, veiled his face, and for three long hours the ribald crew sat shivering in midday midnight.

Meanwhile the earth trembled beneath their feet. The rocks were split and the temple, in superstitious defense of whose perpetuity they had committed the murder of the Just, had its holy veil torn as though by strong invisible hands. The news of this and the feeling of horror produced by the darkness and the earth tremor caused a revulsion of feelings. There were no more gibes and jests, no more thrusting out of tongues and cruel mockeries—they went their way solitary and alone to their homes, or in little silent groups, while each man smote upon his breast in anguish.

Far different was the procession to the gates of Jerusalem from that march of madness which had come out. Observe the power which God has over human minds! See how He can tame the wildest and make the most malicious and proud to cower down at His feet when He does but manifest Himself in the wonders of nature! How much more cowed and terrified will they be when He makes bare His arm and comes forth in the judgments of His wrath to deal with them according to their deeds! This sudden and memorable change in so vast a multitude is the apt representative of two other remarkable mental changes. How like it is to the gracious transformation which a sight of the cross has often worked most blessedly in the hearts of men!

Many have come under the sound of the gospel resolved to scoff, but they have returned to pray. The idlest and even the basest motives have brought men under the preaching, but when Jesus has been lifted up, they have been savingly drawn to Him and, as a consequence, have struck upon their breasts in repentance and gone their way to serve the Savior whom they once blasphemed. Oh, the power—the melting, conquering, transforming power of that dear cross of Christ! My brethren, we have but to abide by the preaching of it. We have but constantly to tell abroad the matchless story, and we may expect to see the most remarkable spiritual results!

We need despair of no man now that Jesus has died for sinners. With such a hammer as the doctrine of the cross, the flintiest heart will be broken! And with such a fire as the sweet love of Christ, the mightiest iceberg will be melted! We need never despair for the heathenish or superstitious races of men. If we can but find occasion to bring the doctrine of Christ crucified into contact with their natures, it will yet change them, and Christ will be their king.

A second and most monumental change is also foretold by the incident in our text, namely, the effect which a sight of Christ enthroned will have upon the proud and obstinate, who in this life rebelled against Him. Here they fearlessly jested concerning Him and insultingly demanded, "Who is the Lord, that we should obey Him?" (See Exodus 5:2.) Here they boldly united in a conspiracy to break His bands asunder and cast His cords from them. (See Psalm 2:3.) But when they wake up at the blast of the trumpet and see the great white throne (see Revelation 20:11–12), which, like a mirror, shall reflect their conduct upon them, what a change will be in their minds!

Where now your quips and your jests? Where now your malicious speeches and your persecuting words? What? Is there not one among you who can play the man and insult the Man of Nazareth to His face? No, not one! Like cowardly dogs they slink away! The infidel's bragging tongue is silent! The proud spirit of the atheist is broken—his blustering and his carping are hushed forever! With shrieks of dismay and clamorous cries of terror, they entreat the hills to cover them and the mountains to conceal them from the face of that very Man whose cross was once the subject of their scorn! O take heed, you sinners, take heed, I pray you, and be you changed this day by divine grace, lest you be changed by and by due to terror, for the heart which will not be bent by the love of Christ shall be broken by the terror of His name!

If Jesus upon the cross does not save you, Christ on the throne shall damn you! If Christ dying is not your life, Christ living shall be your death! If Christ on earth is not your heaven, Christ coming from heaven shall be your hell! O may God's grace work a blessed turning of grace in each of us, that we may not be turned into hell in the dread day of reckoning!

We shall now draw nearer to the text and, in the first place, analyze the general mourning around the cross. Second, we shall, if God shall help us, endeavor to join in the sorrowful chorus. And then, before we conclude, we shall remind you that at the foot of the cross our sorrow must be mingled with joy.

I. ANALYZE THE GENERAL MOURNING

"All the people that came together to that sight, beholding the things which were done, smote their breasts, and returned" (Luke 23:48). They all smote their breasts, but not all from the same cause. They were all afraid, not all for the same reason. The outward manifestations were alike in the whole mass, but the grades of difference in feeling were as many as the minds in which they ruled. There were many, no doubt, who were merely moved with a transient emotion.

They had seen the death agonies of a remarkable Man, and the attendant wonders had persuaded them that He was something more than an ordinary being, and therefore they were afraid. With a kind of indefinite fear, grounded upon no very intelligent reasoning, they were alarmed because God was angry and had closed the eye of day upon them and made the rocks to split. (See Matthew 27:51.) Burdened with this indistinct fear, they went their way home trembling and humbled. But perhaps before the next morning light had dawned, they had forgotten it all, and the next day found them greedy for another bloody spectacle and ready to nail another Christ to the cross, if there had been such another to be found in the land.

Their beating of the breast was not a breaking of the heart. It was an April shower, a dewdrop of the morning, a hoarfrost that dissolved when the sun had risen. Like a shadow the emotion crossed their minds, and like a shadow it left no trace behind. How often, in the preaching of the cross, has this been the only result in tens of thousands! In this house, where so many souls have been converted, many more have shed tears which have been wiped away, and the reason of their tears has been forgotten. A handkerchief has dried up their emotions. Alas! Alas, that while it may be difficult to move men with the story of the cross to weeping, it is even more difficult to make those emotions permanent.

"I have seen something amazing this morning," said one who had listened to a faithful and earnest preacher. "I have seen a whole congregation in tears." "Alas!" said the preacher, "there is something more amazing still, for the most of them will go their way to forget that they ever shed a tear." Ah, my hearers, shall it be always so—always so? Then, O you impenitent, there shall come to your eyes a tear which shall drip forever—a scalding drop which no mercy shall ever wipe away—a thirst that shall never be abated! There shall come to you a worm that shall never die and a fire that never shall be quenched! By the love you bear your souls, I pray you escape from the wrath to come!

Others among that great crowd exhibited emotion based upon more thoughtful reflection. They saw that they had shared in the murder of an innocent person "Alas," they said, "we see through it all now. That Man was no offender. In all that we have ever heard or seen of Him, He did good and only good! He always healed the sick, fed the hungry, and raised the dead. There is not a word of all His teaching that is really contrary to the law of God. He was a pure and holy Man. We have all been duped. Those priests have egged us on to put to death One whom it were a thousand mercies if we could restore to life again at once. Our race has killed its Benefactor."

"Yes," says one, "I thrust out my tongue. I found it almost impossible to restrain myself when everybody else was laughing and mocking at His tortures. But I am afraid I have mocked at the innocent, and I tremble lest the darkness which God has sent was His reprobation of my wickedness in oppressing the innocent." Such feelings would abide, but I can suppose that they might not bring men to sincere repentance—for while they might feel sorry they had oppressed the innocent, yet, perceiving nothing more in Jesus than mere evil-treated virtue and suffering manhood, the natural emotion might soon pass away, and the moral and spiritual result be of no great value.

How frequently have we seen in our hearers that same description of emotion! They have regretted that Christ should be put to death. They have felt like that old king of France who said, "I wish I had been there with 10,000 of my soldiers—I would have cut their throats sooner than they should have touched Him." But those very feelings have been evidence that they did not feel their share in the guilt as they ought to have done and that to them the cross of Jesus was no more a saving spectacle than the death of a common martyr. Dear hearers, beware of making the cross to be a commonplace thing with you! Look beyond the sufferings of the innocent Manhood of Jesus and see upon the cross the atoning sacrifice of Christ, or else you look to the cross in vain.

No doubt there were a few in the crowd who smote upon their breasts because they felt, "We have put to death a Prophet of God. As of old our nation slew Isaiah and put to death others of the Master's servants, so today they have nailed to the cross one of the last of the prophets, and His blood will be upon us and upon our children." Perhaps some of them said, "This Man claimed to be Messiah, and the miracles which attended His death prove that He was so. His life betokens it and His death declares it. What will become of our nation if we have slain the Prince of Peace? How will God visit us if we have put His Prophet to death?"

Such mourning was in advance of other forms. It showed a deeper thought and a clearer knowledge, and it may have been an admirable preparation for the later hearing of the gospel—but it would not of itself suffice as evidence of grace. I shall be glad if my hearers in this house today are persuaded by the character of Christ that He must have been a Prophet sent of God and that He was the Messiah promised of old. And I shall be gratified if they, therefore, lament the shameful cruelties which He received from our apostate race. Such emotions of compunction and pity are most commendable, and under God's blessing they may prove to be the furrow rows of your heart in which the gospel may take root. He who thus was cruelly put to death was God over all blessed forever, the world's Redeemer and the Savior of such as put their trust in Him! May you accept Him today as your Deliverer and so be saved, for if not, the most virtuous regrets concerning His death—however much they may indicate your enlightenment—will not manifest your true conversion.

In the motley company who all went home striking their breasts, let us hope that there were some who said, "Certainly this was the Son of God" (see Matthew 27:54), and mourned to think He should have suffered for their transgressions and been put to grief for their iniquities. Those who came to that point were saved! Blessed were the eyes that looked upon the slaughtered Lamb in such a way as that, and happy were the hearts that then and there were broken because He was bruised and put to grief for their sakes. Beloved, aspire to this! May God's grace bring you to see in Jesus Christ no other than God made flesh, hanging upon the cross in agony to die, the Just for the unjust, that we may be saved!

O come and repose your trust in Him and then strike upon your breasts at the thought that such a Victim should have been necessary for your redemption! Then may you cease to strike your breasts and begin to clap your hands for joy—they who thus bewail a Savior may rejoice in Him, for He is theirs and they are His!

II. JOIN IN THE LAMENTATION. EACH MAN, ACCORDING TO HIS SINCERITY OF HEART, SHOULD NOW BEHOLD THE CROSS AND STRIKE UPON HIS BREAST.

We will by faith put ourselves at the foot of the little knoll of Calvary. There we see in the center, between two thieves, the Son of God made flesh, nailed by His hands and feet and dying in an anguish which words cannot portray. Look well, I pray you. Look steadfastly and devoutly, gazing through your tears. 'Tis He who was worshipped of angels who is now dying for the sons of men!

Sit down and watch the death of Death's Destroyer! I shall ask you first to strike your breasts, as you remember that you see in Him your own sins. How great He is! That crown of thorns is on the head once crowned with all the royalties of heaven and earth! He who dies there is no common man! King of kings and Lord of lords is He who hangs on yonder cross. Then see the greatness of your sins which required so vast a sacrifice. They must be infinite sins to require an infinite person to lay down His life for their removal. You can never compass or comprehend the greatness of your Lord in His essential character and dignity. Neither shall you ever be able to understand the blackness and heinousness of the sin which demanded His life as an atonement.

Brothers and sisters, strike your breast and say, "God be merciful to me, the greatest of sinners, for I am such." (See 1 Timothy 1:15.) Look well into the face of Jesus and see how vile they have made Him! They have stained those cheeks with spit! They have lashed those shoulders with a felon's scourge! They have put Him to the death which was only awarded to the meanest Roman slave! They have hung Him up between heaven and earth as though He were fit for neither! They have stripped Him naked and left Him not a rag to cover Him!

See here, then, O believer, the shame of your sins! What a shameful thing your sins must have been. What a disgraceful and abominable thing, if Christ must be made such a shame for you! O be ashamed of yourself, to think your Lord should thus be scorned and made nothing of for you! See how they aggravate His sorrows! It was not enough to crucify Him—they must insult Him! Nor that enough; they must mock His prayers and turn His dying cries into themes for jest while they offer Him vinegar to drink. See, beloved, how aggravated were your sins and mine!

Come, my brothers and sisters, let us all strike upon our breasts and say, "Oh, how our sins have piled up their guiltiness! It was not merely that we broke the law, but we sinned against light and knowledge. We sinned against rebukes and warnings. As His griefs are aggravated, even so are our sins!" Look still into His dear face and see the lines of anguish which indicate the deeper inward sorrow which far transcends mere bodily pain and suffering. God, His Father, has forsaken Him! God has made Him a curse for us.

Then what must the curse of God have been against us? What must our sins have deserved if, when sin was only imputed to Christ and laid upon Him for a while, His Father turned His head away and made His Son cry out, "*Lama sabachthani!*" (Matthew 27:46)? Oh, what an accursed thing our sin must be, and what a curse would have come upon us! What thunderbolts, what coals of fire, what indignation and wrath from the Most High must have been our portion had not Jesus interposed! If Jehovah did not spare His Son, how little would He have spared guilty, worthless men if He had dealt with us after our sins and rewarded us according to our iniquities!

As we still sit down and look at Jesus, we remember that His death was voluntary—He need not have died unless He had so willed. Here, then, is another striking feature of our sin, for our sin was voluntary, too. We did not sin as of compulsion, but we deliberately chose the evil way. O sinner, let both of us sit down together and tell the Lord that we have no justification, or extenuation, or excuse to offer—we have sinned willfully against light and knowledge, against love and mercy. Let us strike upon our breasts, as we see Jesus willingly suffer and confess that we have willingly offended against the just and righteous laws of a most good and gracious God.

I could gladly keep you looking into those five wounds and studying that marred face and counting every purple drop that flowed from hands and feet and side, but time would fail us. Only that one wound—let it abide with you—strike your breast because you see in Christ your sin. Looking again—changing, as it were, our standpoint, but still keeping our eye upon that same, dear Crucified One—let us see there the neglected and despised remedy for our sin. If sin itself, in its first condition, as rebellion, brings no tears to our eyes, it certainly ought, in its second manifestation, as ingratitude.

The sin of rebellion is vile. But the sin of slighting the Savior is viler still. He that hangs on the cross in groans and griefs unutterable is He whom some of you have never thought of—whom you do not love, to whom you never pray—in whom you place no confidence and whom you never serve. I will not accuse you. I will ask those dear wounds to do it, sweetly and tenderly. I will rather accuse myself, for, alas! Alas, there was a time when I heard of Him as with a deaf ear! There was a time when I was told of Him and understood the love He bore to sinners, and yet my heart was like a stone within me and would not be moved! I stopped my ears and would not be charmed, even with such a master-fascination as the disinterested love of Jesus!

I think if I had been spared to live the life of an ungodly man for thirty, forty, or fifty years and had been converted at last, I should never have been able to blame myself sufficiently for rejecting Jesus during all those years. Why, even those of us who were converted in our youth and almost in our childhood cannot help blaming ourselves to think that so dear a Friend, who had done so much for us, was so long slighted by us! Who could have done more for us than He, since He gave Himself for our sins? Ah, how we did wrong Him while we withheld our hearts from Him! O sinners, how can you keep the doors of your hearts shut against the Friend of sinners? How can we close the door against Him who cries, "My head is wet with dew and My locks with the drops of the night: open to Me, my Beloved, open to Me"? (See Song of Solomon 5:2.)

I am persuaded there are some here who are His elect—you were chosen by Him from before the foundation of the world, and you shall be with Him in heaven one day to sing His praises, and yet, at this moment, though you hear His name, you do not love Him. And though you are told of what He did, you do not trust Him. What? Shall that iron bar always fast close the gate of your heart? Shall that door be always bolted? O Spirit of the living God, win an entrance for the blessed Christ this morning! If anything can do it, surely it must be a sight of the crucified Christ—that matchless spectacle shall make a heart of stone relent and melt, subdued by Jesus's love! O may the Holy Spirit work this gracious melting, and He shall have all the honor!

Still keeping you at the foot of the cross, dear friends, every believer here may well strike upon his breast this morning as he thinks of who it was that smarted so upon the cross. Who was it? It was He who loved us before the world was made! It was He who is this day the Bridegroom of our souls, our Best-Beloved; He who has taken us into the banqueting house and waved His banner of love over us. It is He who has made us one with Himself and has vowed to present us to His Father without spot. (See Ephesians 5:27.) It is He, our Husband, our Ishi (see Hosea 2:16), who has called us His Hephzibah (see Isaiah 62:4) because His soul delights in us. It is He who suffered thus for us.

Suffering does not always excite the same degree of pity. You must know something of the individual before the innermost depths of the soul are stirred, and so it happens to us that the higher the character and the more able we are to appreciate it, the closer the relation and the more fondly we reciprocate the love—the more deeply does suffering strike the soul. You are coming to His table, some of you, today, and you will partake of bread—I pray you remember that it represents the quivering flesh that was filled with pain on Calvary! You will sip of that cup—be sure to remember that it betokens to you the blood of One who loves you better than you could be loved by mother, or by husband, or by friend!

O sit down and strike your breasts that He should grieve! That Heaven's Sun should be eclipsed! That Heaven's Lily should be spotted with blood and Heaven's Rose should be whitened with a deadly pallor! Lament that perfection should be accused, innocence struck, and love murdered—and that Christ, the happy and the holy, the ever blessed, who had been for ages the delight of angels—should now become the sorrowful, the acquaintance of grief, the bleeding and the dying! Smite upon your breasts, believers, and go your way! Beloved in the Lord, if such grief as this should be kindled in you, it will be well to pursue the subject and to reflect upon how unbelieving and how cruel we have been to Jesus since the day that we have known Him.

What? Does He bleed for me, and have I doubted Him? Is He the Son of God, and have I suspected His fidelity? Have I stood at the foot of the cross unmoved? Have I spoken of my dying Lord in a cold, indifferent spirit? Have I ever preached Christ crucified with a dry eye and a heart unmoved? Do I bow my knee in private prayer, and are my thoughts wandering when they ought to be bound hand and foot to His dear, bleeding self? Am I accustomed to turn over the pages of the evangelists which record my Master's wondrous sacrifice, and have I never stained those pages with my tears? Have I never paused spellbound over the sacred sentence which recorded this miracle of miracles, this marvel of marvels?

Oh, shame upon you, hard heart! Well may I strike you! May God strike you with the hammer of His Spirit and break you to shivers! O you stony heart, you granite soul, you flinty spirit— well may I strike the breast which harbors you, to think that I should be so doltish in the presence of love so amazing, so divine! Brethren, you may strike upon your breasts as you look at the cross and mourn that you should have done so little for your Lord. I think if anybody could have sketched my future life in the day of my conversion and had said, "You will be dull and cold in spiritual things, and you will exhibit but little earnestness and little gratitude," I should have said, like Hazael, "*Is your servant a dog, that he should do this great thing?*" (2 Kings 8:13).

I suppose I read your hearts when I say that most of you are disappointed with your own conduct as compared with your too-flattering prophecies of yourselves! What? Am I really pardoned? Am I in very deed washed in that warm stream which gushed from the riven side of Jesus, and yet am I not wholly consecrated to Christ? What? In my body do I bear the marks of the Lord Jesus, and can I live almost without a thought of Him? Am I plucked like a brand from the burning, and have I small care to win others from the wrath to come? Has Jesus stooped to win me, and do I not labor to win others for Him? Was He all in earnest about me, and am I only half in earnest about Him? Dare I waste a minute, dare I trifle away an hour? Have I an evening to spend in vain gossip and idle frivolities?

O my heart, well may I strike you that, at the sight of the death of the dear Lover of my soul, I should not be fired by the highest zeal and be impelled by the most ardent love to a perfect conse-cration of every power of my nature, every affection of my spirit, every faculty of my whole man! This mournful strain might be pursued to far greater lengths. We might follow up our confes-sions, still striking, still accusing, still regretting, still bewailing. We might continue upon the bass notes evermore, and yet might we not express sufficient contrition for the shameful manner in which we have treated our blessed Friend. We might say with one of our hymn writers:

> Lord, let me weep for nothing but sin,
> And after none but You.
> And then I would—O that I might
> A constant weeper be!

III. AT CALVARY, DOLOROUS NOTES ARE NOT THE ONLY SUITABLE MUSIC

We admired our poet when, in the hymn which we have just sung, he appears to question with himself which would be the most fitting tune for Golgotha:

> "It is finished"; shall we raise
> Songs of sorrow or of praise?
> Mourn to see the Savior die,
> Or proclaim His victory?
> If of Calvary we tell,
> How can songs of triumph swell?
> If of man redeemed from woe,
> How shall notes of mourning flow?

He shows that since our sin pierced the side of Jesus, there is cause for unlimited lamentation, but since the blood which flowed from the wound has cleansed our sin, there is ground for unbounded thanksgiving! And, therefore, the poet, after having balanced the matter in a few verses, concludes:

"It is finished," let us raise
Songs of thankfulness and praise.

After all, you and I are not in the same condition as the multitude who had surrounded Calvary, for at that time our Lord was still dead—now He is risen, indeed! There were yet three days from that Thursday evening (for there is much reason to believe that our Lord was not crucified on Friday), in which Jesus must dwell in the regions of the dead. Our Lord, therefore, so far as human eyes could see Him, was a proper object of pity and mourning and not of thanksgiving.

But now, beloved, He ever lives and gloriously reigns! No grave confines that blessed body! He saw no corruption, for the moment when the third day dawned, He could no longer be held with the bonds of death, but He manifested Himself alive unto His disciples! He tarried in this world for forty days. Some of His time was spent with those who knew Him in the flesh. Perhaps a larger part of it was passed with those saints who came out of their graves after His resurrection, but certain it is that He is gone up, as the first-fruit from the dead. He is gone up to the right hand of God, even the Father!

Do not bewail those wounds—they are lustrous with supernal splendor! Do not lament His death—He lives no more to die! Do not mourn that shame and spitting:

The head that once was crowned with thorns
Is crowned with glory now.

Look up and thank God that death has no more dominion over Him. He ever lives to make intercession for us (see Hebrews 7:25), and He shall shortly come with angelic bands surrounding Him to judge the quick and the dead. The argument for joy overshadows the reason for sorrow! Like as a woman when the child is born remembers no more her anguish, for joy that a child is born into the world, so, in the thought of the risen Savior who has taken possession of His crown, we will forget the lamentation of the cross and the sorrows of the broken heart of Calvary. (See John 16:21–22.)

Moreover, hear the shrill voice of the high-sounding cymbals and let your hearts rejoice within you, for in His death our Redeemer conquered all the hosts of hell. They came against Him furiously, yes, they came against Him to eat up His flesh, but they stumbled and fell. They compassed Him about, yes, they compassed Him about like bees, but in the name of the Lord did the Champion destroy them! Against the whole multitude of sins and all the battalions of the pit, the Savior stood, a solitary soldier fighting against innumerable bands, but He has slain them all! "Bruised is the dragon's head." Jesus has led captivity captive! He conquered when He fell! And let the notes of victory drown forever the cries of sorrow!

Moreover, brothers and sisters, let it be remembered that men have been saved! Let there stream before your gladdened eyes this morning the innumerable company of the elect. Robed in white, they come in long procession—they come from distant lands, from every clime. They were once scarlet with sin and black with iniquity; they are now all white and pure, and without spot before the throne forever. They are beyond temptation, beatified and made like Jesus! And how? It was all through Calvary. There was their sin put away! There was their everlasting righteousness brought in and consummated! Let the hosts that are before the throne, as they wave their palms and touch their golden harps, excite you to a joy like their own, and let that celestial music hush the gentler voices which mournfully exclaim:

> Alas, and did my Savior bleed?
> And did my Sovereign die?
> Would He devote that sacred head
> For such a worm as I?

Nor is that all. You yourself are saved! O believer, this will always be one of your greatest joys, that others are converted through your instrumentality! This is occasion for much thanksgiving, but your Savior's advice to you is, *"Notwithstanding in this rejoice not, that the spirits are subject to you; but rather rejoice, because your names are written in heaven"* (Luke 10:20). You, a spirit meet to be cast away! You whose portion must have been with devils—you are this day forgiven, adopted, saved, on the road to heaven! Oh, while you think that you are saved from hell, that you are lifted up to glory, you cannot but rejoice that your sin is put away from you through the death of Jesus Christ, your Lord!

Lastly, there is one thing which we ought always to remember with joy regarding Christ's death, and that is that although the crucifixion of Jesus was intended to be a blow at the honor and glory of our God—though in the death of Christ the world did, so far as it was able, put God Himself to death and so earn for itself that hideous title, "a deicidal world"—yet never did God have such honor and glory as He obtained through the sufferings of Jesus! Oh, they thought to scorn Him, but they lifted His name on high!

They thought that God was dishonored when He was most glorified! The image of the invisible (see Colossians 1:15)—had they not marred it? The express image of the Father's Person— had they not defiled it? Ah, so they said! But He that sits in the heavens may well laugh and have them in derision (see Psalm 2:4), for what did they do? They did but break the alabaster box, and all the blessed drops of infinite mercy streamed forth to perfume all worlds! They did but rend the veil, and then the glory which had been hidden between the cherubim shone forth upon all lands!

O nature, adoring God with your ancient and priestly mountains, extolling Him with your trees which clap their hands, and worshipping with your seas which, in their fullness, roar out Jehovah's praise! With all your tempests and flames of fire, your dragons, and your deeps, your snow, and your hail—you cannot glorify God as Jesus glorified Him when He became obedient unto death! O heaven, with all your jubilant angels, your ever-chanting cherubim and seraphim, your thrice-holy hymns, your streets of gold and endless harmonies—you cannot reveal the deity as Jesus Christ revealed it on the cross!

O hell, with all your infinite horrors, and flames unquenchable, and pains, and griefs, and shrieks of tortured ghosts! Even you cannot reveal the justice of God as Christ revealed it in His riven heart upon the bloody cross! O earth, and heaven, and hell! O time, and eternity, things present, and things to come, visible and invisible—you are dim mirrors of the Godhead compared with the bleeding Lamb! O heart of God, I see You nowhere as at Golgotha, where the Word Incarnate reveals the justice and the love, the holiness and the tenderness, of God in one blaze of glory! If any created mind would gladly see the glory of God, he need not gaze upon the starry skies, nor soar into the heaven of heavens! He has but to bow at the foot of the cross and watch the crimson streams which gush from Emmanuel's wounds!

If you would behold the glory of God, you need not gaze between the gates of pearls. You have but to look beyond the gates of Jerusalem and see the Prince of Peace expire. If you would receive the most noble conception that ever filled the human mind of the loving-kindness and the greatness, and the pity, and yet the justice and the severity and the wrath of God, you need not lift up your eyes, nor cast them down, nor look to paradise, nor gaze on

Tophet—you have but to look into the heart of Christ all crushed and broken and bruised, and you have seen it all!

Oh, the joy that springs from the fact that God has triumphed after all! Death is not the victor! Evil is not master! There are not two rival kingdoms, one governed by the God of good and the other by the god of evil—no, evil is bound, chained, and led captive! Its sinews are cut, its head is broken! Its king is bound to the dread chariot of Jehovah-Jesus, and as the white horses of triumph drag the Conqueror up the everlasting hills in splendor of glory, the monsters of the pit cringe at His chariot wheels!

Therefore, beloved, we close this discourse with this sentence of humble yet joyful worship: "Glory be unto the Father and to the Son and to the Holy Spirit: as it was in the beginning, is now, and ever shall be, world without end. Amen."

4

CHRIST MADE A CURSE FOR US

"Christ has redeemed us from the curse of the law,
being made a curse for us: for it is written,
Cursed is every one that hangs on a tree."
—Galatians 3:13

The apostle Paul had been showing to the Galatians that salvation is in no degree by works. He proved this all-important truth of God, in the verses which precede the text, by a very conclusive form of double reasoning. He showed, first, that the law could not give the blessing of salvation, for, since all had broken it, all that the law could do was to curse. He quoted the substance of the twenty-seventh chapter of Deuteronomy when he wrote, *"Cursed is every one that continues not in all things which are written in the book of the law to do them"* (Galatians 3:10). And as no man can claim that he has continued in all things that are in the law, Paul pointed out the clear inference that all men under the law had incurred the curse.

He then reminded the Galatians, in the second place, that if any had ever been blessed in the olden times, the blessing came not by the law but by their faith—and to prove this, he quoted a passage from Habakkuk in which it is distinctly stated that the just shall live by faith (see Habakkuk 2:4)—so that those who were just and righteous did not live before God on the footing of their obedience to the law, but they were justified and made to live on the ground of their being believers. See, then, that if the law inevitably curses us all, and if the only people who are said to have been preserved in gracious life were justified not by works but by faith, then is it certain beyond a doubt that the salvation and justification of a sinner cannot be by the works of the law but altogether by the grace of God through faith which is in Christ Jesus.

But the apostle Paul, no doubt feeling that, now he was declaring that doctrine, he had better declare the foundation and root of it, unveiled in the text before us a reason why men are not saved by their personal righteousness but are saved by their faith. He told us that the reason is this: that men are not saved by any personal merit; their salvation lies in another—lies, in fact, in Christ Jesus, the representative Man who alone can deliver us from the curse which the law brought upon us. And since works do not connect us with Christ, but faith is the uniting bond, faith becomes the way of salvation. (See Galatians 3:11–13.)

Since faith is the hand that lays hold upon the finished work of Christ—which works could not and would not do, for works lead us to boast and to forget Christ (see Ephesians 2:8–9)—faith becomes the true and only way of obtaining justification and everlasting life. In order that such faith may be nurtured in us, may God the Holy Spirit this morning lead us into the depths of the great work of Christ! May we understand more clearly the nature of His substitution and of the suffering which it entailed upon Him. Let us see, indeed, the truth of the stanzas whose music has just died away:

He bore that we might never bear
His Father's righteous ire.

I. WHAT IS THE CURSE OF THE LAW HERE INTENDED?

It is the curse of God. God, who made the law, has appended certain penal consequences to the breaking of it, and the man who violates the law becomes at once the subject of the wrath of the Lawgiver. It is not the curse of the mere law of itself—it is a curse from the great Lawgiver whose arm is strong to defend His statutes. Therefore, at the very outset of our reflections, let us be assured that the curse of the law must be supremely just and morally unavoidable.

It is not possible that our God, who delights to bless us, should inflict an atom of curse upon any one of His creatures unless the highest right shall require it. And if there is any method by which holiness and purity can be maintained without a curse, rest assured the God of love will not imprecate sorrow upon His creatures. The curse, then, if it falls, must be a necessary one—in its very essence necessary for the preservation of order in the universe and for the manifestation of the holiness of the universal Sovereign.

Be assured, too, that when God curses, it is a curse of the weightiest kind. The curse causeless shall not come, but God's curses are never causeless, and they come home to offenders with overwhelming power. Sin must be punished, and when, by long continuance and impenitence in evil, God is provoked to speak the malediction, I know that he whom He curses is cursed, indeed. There is something so terrible in the very idea of the omnipotent God pronouncing a curse upon a transgressor that my blood curdles at it, and I cannot express myself very clearly or even coherently. A father's curse, how terrible! But what is that to the malediction of the great Father of spirits?

To be cursed of men is no mean evil, but to be accursed of God is terror and dismay! Sorrow and anguish lie in that curse! Death is involved in it, as is that second death which John foresaw in Patmos and described as being cast into a lake of fire. (See Revelation 20:14.) Hear the Word of the Lord by His servant Nahum and consider what His curse must be:

> God is jealous, and the LORD revenges; the LORD revenges, and is furious; the LORD will take vengeance on His adversaries, and He reserves wrath for His enemies....The mountains quake at Him, and the hills melt, and the earth is burned at His presence, yea, the world, and all that dwell therein. Who can stand before His indignation? and who can abide in the fierceness of His anger? His fury is poured out like fire, and the rocks are thrown down by Him. (Nahum 1:2, 5–6)

Remember, also, the prophecy of Malachi: *For, behold, the day comes, that shall burn as an oven; and all the proud, yea, and all that do wickedly, shall be stubble: and the day that comes shall burn them up, says the LORD of hosts, that it shall leave them neither root nor branch*" (Malachi 4:1). Let such words—and there are many like they—sink into your hearts, that you may fear and tremble before this just and holy Lord! If we would look further into the meaning of the curse that arises from the breach of the law, we must remember that a curse is, first of all, a sign of displeasure.

Now, we learn from Scripture that God is angry with the wicked every day. (See Psalm 7:11.) Though toward the persons of sinners God exhibits great longsuffering, yet sin exceedingly provokes His holy mind. (See Exodus 34:6–7.) Sin is a thing so utterly loathsome and detestable to the purity of the Most High that no thought of evil, or ill word, or unjust action, is tolerated by Him. He observes every sin, and His holy soul is stirred thereby. He is of purer eyes than to behold iniquity. He cannot endure it. He is a God that will certainly execute vengeance upon every evil work. A curse implies something more than mere anger. It is suggested by burning indignation, and truly our God is not only somewhat angry with sinners, but His wrath is great toward sin.

Wherever sin exists, there the fullness of the power of the divine indignation is directed. And though the effect of that wrath may be, for a while, restrained through abundant longsuffering, yet God is greatly indignant with the iniquities of men. We wink at sin, yes, and even harden our hearts till we laugh at it and take pleasure in it. But, oh, let us not think that God is such as we are! Let us not suppose that sin can be beheld by Him and yet no indignation be felt. Ah, no, the most holy God has written warnings in His Word which plainly inform us how terribly He is provoked by iniquity, as, for instance, when He says…

Now consider this, you that forget God, lest I tear you in pieces, and there be none to deliver.   (Psalm 50:22)

Therefore says the Lord, the Lord of hosts, the mighty One of Israel, Ah, I will ease Me of My adversaries, and avenge Me of My enemies.   (Isaiah 1:24)

For we know Him that has said, Vengeance belongs to Me, I will recompense, says the Lord. And again, the Lord shall judge His people. It is a fearful thing to fall into the hands of the living God.   (Hebrews 10:30–31)

Moreover, a curse imprecates evil and is, as it comes from God, of the nature of a threat. It is as though God should say, "By and by I will visit you for this offense. You have broken My law, which is just and holy, and the inevitable penalty shall certainly come upon you."

Now, God has throughout His Word given many such curses as these—He has threatened men over and over again. *"If he turn not, He will whet his sword; He has bent His bow, and made it ready"* (Psalm 7:12). Sometimes the threat is wrapped up in a plaintive lamentation: *"Turn you, turn you from your evil ways; for why will you die, O house of Israel?"* (Ezekiel 33:11). But still it is plain and clear that God will not suffer sin to go unpunished—and when the fullness of time shall come and the measure shall be filled to the brim and the weight of iniquity shall be fully reached and the harvest shall be ripe, and the cry of wickedness shall come up mightily into the ears of the Lord God of Sabaoth—then will He come forth in robes of vengeance and overwhelm His adversaries.

But God's curse is something more than a threat. He comes at length to blows. He uses warning words at first, but sooner or later He bares His sword for execution. The curse of God, as to its actual infliction, may be guessed at by some occasions where it has been seen on earth. Look at Cain, a wanderer, and a vagabond upon the face of the earth! (See Genesis 4:12.) Read the curse that Jeremiah pronounced by the command of God upon Pashur: *"Behold, I will make you a terror to yourself, and to all your friends: and they shall fall by the sword of their enemies, and your eyes shall behold it"* (Jeremiah 20:4.) Or, if you would behold the curse upon a larger scale, remember the day when the huge floodgates of earth's deepest fountains were loosed, and the waters leaped up from their habitations like lions eager for their prey! (See Genesis 7:10–12.)

Remember the day of vengeance when the windows of heaven were opened and the great deep above the firmament was confused with the deep that is beneath the firmament, and all flesh were swept away—except only the few who were hidden in the ark which God's covenant mercy had prepared. Consider that dreadful day when sea monsters whelped and stabled in the palaces of ancient kings! When millions of sinners sank to rise no more! When universal ruin flew with raven wings over a shoreless sea vomited from the mouth of death! Then was the curse of God poured out upon the earth! (See Genesis 7:15–24).

Look yet again, further down in time. Stand with Abraham at his tent door and see toward the east the sky all red at early morning with a glare that came not from the sun—sheets of flames went up to heaven and were met by showers of yet more vivid fire descending from the skies. Sodom and Gomorrah, having given themselves up to strange flesh, received the curse of God, and hell was rained upon them out of heaven until they were utterly consumed. (See Genesis 19:1–29.)

If you would see another form of the curse of God, remember that bright spirit who once stood as servitor in heaven—the son of the morning, one of the chief angels of God! (See Isaiah 14:12.) Think how he lost his lofty principality when sin entered into him! See how an archangel became an archfiend and Satan, who is called Apollyon, and fell from his lofty throne (see Luke 10:18), banished forever from peace and happiness—to wander through dry places, seeking rest and finding none (see Matthew 12:43)—to be reserved in chains of darkness unto the judgment of the Last Great Day. Such was the curse that it withered an angel into a devil! It burned up the cities of the plain! It swept away the population of the globe!

Nor have you yet the full idea. There is a place of woe and horror—a land of darkness as darkness itself and of the shadow of death—without any order and where the light is darkness. There those miserable spirits who have refused repentance and have hardened themselves against the Most High are forever banished from their God and from all hope of peace or restoration. If your ear could be applied to the gratings of their cells—if you could walk the gloomy corridors wherein damned spirits are confined— you would, then, with chilled blood and hair erect, learn what the curse of the law must be—that dread malediction which comes on the disobedient from the hand of the just and righteous God!

The curse of God is to lose God's favor and, consequently, to lose the blessings which come upon that blessing: to lose peace of mind, to lose hope, ultimately to lose life itself—for *"the soul that sins, it shall die"* (Ezekiel 18:20). And that loss of life and being cast into eternal death is the most terrible of all, consisting in, as it does, everlasting separation from God and everything that makes existence truly life. It is a destruction lasting forever. According to the scriptural description of it, it is the fruit of the curse of the law.

Oh, heavy tidings have I to deliver this day to some of you! Hard is my task to have to testify to you the terrible justice of the law! But you would not understand or prize the exceeding love of Christ if you heard not the curse from which He delivers His people. Therefore hear me patiently! O unhappy men—unhappy men who are under God's curse today! You may dress yourselves in scarlet and fine linen. You may go to your feasts and drain your full bowls of wine. You may lift high the sparkling cup and whirl in the joyous dance, but if God's curse is on you, what madness possesses you! O sirs, if you could but see it and understand it, this curse would darken all the windows of your mirth!

O that you could hear, for once, the voice which speaks against you from Ebal, with doleful repetition:

> *Cursed shall you be in the city, and cursed shall you be in the field. Cursed shall be your basket and your store. Cursed shall be the fruit of your body, and the fruit of your land, the increase of your cattle and the flocks of your sheep. Cursed shall you be when you come in, and cursed shall you be when you go out.* (Deuteronomy 28:16–18)

How is it that you can rest while such sentences pursue you? Oh, unhappiest of men are those who pass out of this life still accursed! One might weep tears of blood to think of them! Let our thoughts fly to them for a moment, but, O, let us not continue in sin, lest our spirits be condemned to hold perpetual companionship in their grief! Let us fly to the dear cross of Christ, where the curse was put away, that we may never come to know, in the fullness of its horror, what the curse may mean!

II. WHO ARE UNDER THIS CURSE?

Listen with solemn awe, O sons of men! First, especially, and foremost, the Jewish nation lies under the curse, for such I gather from the connection. To them the law of God was very peculiarly given beyond all others. (See Exodus 19:5–6.) They heard it from Sinai (see Exodus 19–23), and it was to them surrounded with a golden setting of ceremonial symbols and enforced by solemn national covenant. (See Exodus 24–25.)

Moreover, there was a word in the commencement of that law which showed that in a certain sense it peculiarly belonged to Israel: *"I am the Lord your God, which have brought you out of the land of Egypt, out of the house of bondage"* (Exodus 20:2.)

Paul told us that those who have sinned without law shall be punished without law. (See Romans 2:12.) But the Jewish nation, having received the law, if they broke it would become peculiarly liable to the curse which was threatened for such breach. Yet further, all nations that dwell upon the face of the earth are also subject to this curse for this reason—that if the law were not given to all from Sinai, it has been written by the finger of God, more or less legibly, upon the conscience of all mankind. (See Romans 2:14–15.) It needs no prophet to tell humanity that we must not steal—our own judgment so instructs us. There is that within every man which ought to convince him that idolatry is folly, that adultery and unchastity are villainies, that theft and murder and covetousness are all evil.

Now, inasmuch as all men, in some degree, have the law within, to that degree they are under the law. The curse of the law for transgression comes upon them. Moreover, there are some in this house this morning who are peculiarly under the curse. The apostle Paul said, *"As many as are of the works of the law are under the curse"* (Galatians 3:10). Now, there are some of you who choose to be under the law—you deliberately choose to be judged by it. How so? Why, you are trying to reach a place in heaven by your own good works! You are clinging to the idea that something you can do can save you! You have therefore elected to be under the law, and by so doing, you have chosen the curse—for all that the law of works can do for you is to leave you still accursed—because you have not fulfilled all its commands. O sirs, repent of so foolish a choice, and declare from now on that you are willing to be saved by divine grace and not at all by the works of the law!

There is a little band here who feel the weight of the law, to whom I turn with brightest hope, though they themselves are in despair. They feel in their consciences today that they deserve from God the severest punishment. This sense of His wrath weighs them to the dust. I am glad of this, for it is only when we come consciously and penitently under the curse that we accept the way of escape from it. You do not know what it is to be redeemed from the curse till you have first felt the slavery of it. No man will ever rejoice in the liberty which Christ gives him till he has first felt the iron of bondage entering into his soul.

I know there are some here who say, "Let God say what He will against me, or do what He will to me; I deserve it all. If He drives me forever from His presence, and I hear the Judge pronounce that awful sentence, 'Depart, accursed one' (see Matthew 25:41), I can only admit that such has been my heart, and such my life, that I could expect no other doom." O you dear heart, if you are thus brought down, you will listen gladly to me while I now come to a far brighter theme than all this! You are under the curse as you now are, but I rejoice to tell you that the curse has been removed through Jesus Christ our Lord! O may the Lord lead you to see the plan of substitution and to rejoice in it!

III. HOW WAS CHRIST MADE A CURSE FOR US?

The whole pith and marrow of the religion of Christianity lies in the doctrine of "substitution," and I hesitate not to affirm my conviction that a very large proportion of Christians are not Christians at all, for they do not understand the fundamental doctrine of the Christian creed. And, alas, there are preachers who do not preach or even believe this cardinal truth. They speak of the blood of Jesus in an indistinct kind of way and descant upon the death of Christ in a hazy style of poetry, but they do not strike this nail on the head and lay it down that the way of salvation is by Christ's becoming a Substitute for guilty man! This shall make me the plainer and more definite. Sin is an accursed thing. God, from the necessity of His holiness, must curse it. He must punish men for committing it. But the Lord's Christ, the glorious Son of the everlasting Father, became a Man and suffered, in His own proper person the curse which was due to the sons of men, that so by a vicarious offering, God, having been just in punishing sin, could extend His bounteous mercy toward those who believe in the Substitute.

Now for this point. But you enquire, how was Jesus Christ a curse? We beg you to observe the word "made." "He was made a curse." Christ was no curse in Himself. In His person He was spotlessly innocent, and nothing of sin could belong personally to Him. In Him was no sin. *"He has made Him to be sin for us..."*— and Paul expressly added—*"...who knew no sin"* (2 Corinthians 5:21). There must never be supposed to be any degree of blameworthiness or censure in the person or character of Christ as He stands as an individual. He is in that respect without spot or wrinkle or any such thing—the immaculate Lamb of God's Passover.

Nor was Christ made a curse of necessity. There was no necessity in Himself that He should ever suffer the curse—no necessity except that which His own loving suretyship created. His own intrinsic holiness kept Him from sin, and that same holiness kept Him from the curse. He was made sin for us, not on His own account—not with any view to Himself—but wholly because He loved us and chose to put Himself in the place which we ought to have occupied. He was made a curse for us, not, again, I say, out of any personal want or out of any personal necessity, but because He had voluntarily undertaken to be the covenant head of His people and to be their representative and, as their representative, to bear the curse which was due to them.

And then, again, we must emphasize the words "for us"—not on His own account at all but entirely out of love for us, that we might be redeemed. He stood in the sinner's place and was reckoned to be a sinner and treated as a sinner and made a curse for us.

Let us go farther into this truth of God. How was Christ made a curse? In the first place, He was made a curse because all the sins of His people were actually laid on Him. Remember the words of the apostle Paul—it is no doctrine of mine, mark you, it is an inspired sentence, it is God's doctrine: *"He has made Him to be sin for us"* (2 Corinthians 5:21).

And let me note another passage from the prophet Isaiah: *"The Lord has laid on Him the iniquity of us all"* (Isaiah 53:6). And yet another from Isaiah, *"He shall bear their iniquities"* (Isaiah 53:11). The sins of God's people were lifted from off them and imputed to Christ—and their sins were looked upon as if Christ had committed them. He was regarded as if He had been the sinner! He actually and in very deed stood in the sinner's place. Next to the imputation of sin came the curse of sin. The law, looking for sin to punish, with its quick eye detected sin laid upon Christ, and, as it must curse sin wherever it was found, it cursed the sin as it was laid on Christ. So, Christ was made a curse.

Wonderful and awful words; but, as they are scriptural words, we must receive them. Sin being on Christ, the curse came on Christ, and in consequence our Lord felt an unutterable horror of soul. Surely it was that horror which made Him sweat great drops of blood (see Luke 22:44) when He saw and felt that God was beginning to treat Him as if He had been a sinner. The holy soul of Christ shrunk with deepest agony from the slightest contact with sin. So pure and perfect was our Lord that never an evil thought had crossed His mind, nor had His soul been stained by the glances of evil. And yet He stood in God's sight a sinner, and therefore a solemn horror fell upon His soul.

The heart refused its healthful action, and a bloody sweat bedewed his face. Then He began to be made a curse for us, nor did He cease till He had suffered all the penalty which was due on our account. We have been accustomed in divinity to divide the penalty into two parts: the penalty of loss and the penalty of actual suffering. Christ endured both of these. It was due to sinners that they should lose God's favor and presence, and therefore Jesus cried, *"My God, My God, why have You forsaken Me?"* (Matthew 27:46). It was due to sinners that they should lose all personal comfort—Christ was deprived of every consolation; even the last rag of clothing was torn from Him, and He was left like Adam, naked and forlorn. It was necessary that the soul should lose everything that could sustain it, and so did Christ lose every comfortable thing. He looked, and there was no man to pity or help. He was made to cry, *"But I am a worm, and no man; a reproach of men, and despised of the people"* (Psalm 22:6).

As for the second part of the punishment, namely, an actual infliction of suffering, our Lord endured this, also, to the uttermost, as the evangelists clearly show. You have read full often the story of His bodily sufferings. Take care that you never depreciate them. There was an amount of physical pain endured by our Savior which His body never could have borne unless it had been sustained and strengthened by union with His Godhead. Yet the sufferings of His soul were the soul of His sufferings. That soul of His endured a torment equivalent to hell itself. The punishment that was due to the wicked was that of hell, and though Christ suffered not hell, He suffered an equivalent of it.

And now, can your minds conceive what that must have been? It was an anguish never to be measured, an agony never to be comprehended. It is to God, and God alone, that His griefs were fully known. Well does the Greek liturgy put it: "Your unknown sufferings," for they must forever remain beyond guess of human imagination. See, brothers and sisters, Christ has gone thus far—He has taken the sin, taken the curse, and suffered all the penalty. The last penalty of sin was death, and therefore the Redeemer died. Behold, the mighty Conqueror yields up His life upon the tree! His side is pierced! The blood and water flow forth, and His disciples lay His body in the tomb. (See John 19:34, 41–42.)

As He was first numbered with the transgressors (see Isaiah 53:12), He was afterward numbered with the dead. See, beloved, here is Christ bearing the curse instead of His people. Here He is, coming under the load of their sin, and God does not spare Him but smites Him as He must have struck us. He lays His full vengeance on Him. He launches all His thunderbolts against Him. He bids the curse wreak itself upon Him, and Christ suffers all, sustains all.

IV. WHAT ARE THE BLESSED CONSEQUENCES OF CHRIST'S HAVING THUS BEEN MADE A CURSE FOR US?

The consequences are that He has redeemed us from the curse of the law. As many as Christ died for, those are forever free from the curse of the law. For when the law comes to curse a man who believes in Christ, he says, "What have I to do with you, O law? You say, 'I will curse you,' but I reply, 'You have cursed Christ instead of me. Can you curse twice for one offense?'"

Behold how the law is silenced! God's law, having received all it can demand, is not so unrighteous as to demand anything more. All that God can demand of a believing sinner, Christ has already paid, and there is no voice in earth or heaven that can accuse a soul that believes in Jesus. You were in debt, but a Friend paid your debt! No writ can be served on you. It matters nothing that you did not pay it; it is paid, and you have the receipt. That is sufficient in any court of equity. So, with all the penalty that was due to us, Christ has borne it. It is true I have not borne it—I have not been to hell and suffered the full wrath of God—but Christ has suffered that wrath for me, and I am as clear as if I had myself paid the debt to God and had myself suffered His wrath.

Here is a glorious foundation to rest upon! Here is a rock upon which to lay the foundation of eternal comfort! Let a man once get to this—my Lord outside the city's gate, bleeding and dying for me as my surety on the cross—He discharged my debt. Why, then, great God, Your thunders I no longer fear! How can You strike me now? You have exhausted the quiver of Your wrath—every arrow has been already shot forth against the person of my Lord, and I am in Him clear and clean and absolved and delivered—even as if I had never sinned! *"Christ has redeemed us"* (Galatians 3:13), says the text.

How often I have heard certain gentry of the modern school of theology sneer at the atonement, because they charge us with the notion of it being a sort of business transaction, or what they choose to call "the mercantile view of it." I hesitate not to say that the mercantile metaphor expresses rightly God's view of redemption, for we find it so in Scripture. The atonement is a ransom—that is to say, a price paid. And in the present case, the original word is more than usually expressive—it is a payment for, a price instead of.

Jesus did, in His sufferings, perform what may be forcibly and fitly described as the payment of a ransom, the giving to justice, a *quid pro quo* for what was due on our behalf for our sins. Christ, in His person, suffered what we ought to have suffered in our persons. The sins that were ours were made His—He stood as a sinner in God's sight, though not a sinner in Himself. He was punished as a sinner and died as a sinner upon the tree of the curse. Then, having exhausted His imputed sinnership by bearing the full penalty, He made an end of sin and rose again from the dead to bring in that everlasting righteousness which at this moment covers the persons of all His elect, so that they can exultingly cry, "*Who shall lay any thing to the charge of God's elect? It is God that justifies. Who is he that condemns? It is Christ that died, yea rather, that is risen again, who is even at the right hand of God, who also makes intercession for us*" (Romans 8:33–34).

Another blessing flows from this satisfactory substitution. It is this, that now the blessing of God, which had been up to then arrested by the curse, is made most freely to flow. Read the verse that follows the text: "*That the blessing of Abraham might come on the Gentiles through Jesus Christ; that we might receive the promise of the Spirit through faith*" (Galatians 3:14). The blessing of Abraham was that in his seed all nations of the earth should be blessed. (See Genesis 22:18). Since our Lord Jesus Christ has taken away the curse due to sin, a great rock has been lifted out from the river-bed of God's mercy, and the living stream comes rippling, roiling, swelling on in crystal tides—sweeping before it all human sin and sorrow and making glad the thirsty who stoop down to drink there.

O my brothers and sisters, the blessings of God's grace are full and free this morning! They are as full as your necessities. Great sinners, there is great mercy for you! They are as free as your poverty could desire them to be, free as the air you breathe or as the cooling stream that flows along the water brook. You have but to trust Christ, and you shall live! Be you who you may, or what you may, or where you may—though at hell's dark door you lie down to despair and die—yet the message comes to you: God has made Christ to be a propitiation for sin. (See Romans 3:25.) *"He has made Him to be sin for us, who knew no sin; that we might be made the righteousness of God in Him"* (2 Corinthians 5:21). Christ has delivered us from the curse of the law, being made a curse for us.

He that believes has no curse upon him. He may have been an adulterer, a swearer, a drunkard, a murderer; but the moment he believes, God sees none of those sins in him! He sees him as an innocent man and regards his sins as having been laid on the Redeemer and punished in Jesus as He died on the tree. I tell you, if you believe in Christ this morning, my hearer, though you are the most damnable of wretches that ever polluted the earth, yet you shall not have a sin remaining on you after believing! God will look at you as pure! Even omniscience shall not detect a sin in you, for your sin shall be put on the Scapegoat, even Christ, and carried away into forgetfulness so that if your transgression is searched for, it shall not be found. (See Isaiah 43:25; Hebrews 8:12.)

If you believe—there is the question—you are clean! If you will trust the incarnate God, you are delivered! He that believes is justified from all things. *"Believe on the LORD Jesus Christ, and you shall be saved"* (Acts 16:31), for *"he that believes and is baptized shall be saved: but he that believes not shall be damned"* (Mark 16:16).

I have preached to you the gospel—God knows with what a weight upon my soul, and yet with what holy joy! This is no subject for gaudy eloquence and for high-flying attempts at oratory. This is a matter to be put to you plainly and simply. Sinners, you must either be cursed of God, or else you must accept Christ as bearing the curse instead of you. I do beseech you, as you love your souls, if you have any sanity left, accept this blessed and divinely appointed way of salvation! This is the truth of God which the apostles preached, suffered, and died to maintain. It is this for which the reformers struggled. It is this for which the martyrs burned at Smithfield. It is the grand basic doctrine of the Reformation and the very truth of God.

Down with your crosses and rituals! Down with your pretensions to good works and your crouching at the feet of priests to ask absolution from them! Away with your accursed and idolatrous dependence upon yourself! Christ has finished salvation-work— altogether finished it! Hold not up your rags in competition with His fair white linen; Christ has borne the curse. Bring not your pitiful penances and your tears all full of filth to mingle with the precious fountain flowing with His blood! Lay down what is your own, and come and take what is Christ's! Put away, now, everything that you have thought of being or doing by way of winning acceptance with God. Humble yourselves and take Jesus Christ to be the Alpha and Omega, the first and last, the beginning and end of your salvation.

If you do this, not only shall you be saved, but you are saved! Rest, you weary one, for your sins are forgiven. Rise, you lame man, lame through lack of faith, for your transgression is covered. Rise from the dead, you corrupt one, rise, like Lazarus from the tomb (see John 11:43–44), for Jesus calls you! Believe and live. The words in themselves, by the Holy Spirit, are soul-quickening. Have done with your tears of repentance and your vows of good living until you have come to Christ. Then take them up as you will.

Your first lesson should be none but Jesus, none but Jesus, none but Jesus! O come to Him! See, He hangs upon the cross. His arms are open wide, and He cannot close them, for the nails hold them fast. He tarries for you. His feet are fastened to the wood, as though He meant to tarry, still. O come to Him! His heart has room for you. It streams with blood and water—it was pierced for you. That mingled stream is...

Of sin the double cure,
To cleanse you from its guilt and power.

An act of faith will bring you to Jesus. Say, "Lord, I believe; help my unbelief" (see Mark 9:24). And if you do so, He cannot cast you out, for His Word is, *"Him that comes to Me I will in no wise cast out"* (John 6:37).

I have delivered to you the weightiest truth of God that ever ears heard or that lips spoke—put it not from you! As we shall meet each other at the last tremendous day, when heaven and earth are on a blaze and the trumpet shall ring and raise the dead—as we shall meet each other then, I challenge you not to put this from you. If you do, it is at your own peril, and your blood is on your own heads. I plead with you to accept the gospel I have delivered to you. It is Jehovah's gospel. Heaven itself speaks in the words you hear today! Accept Jesus Christ as your Substitute. O do it now, this moment, and God shall have glory, but you shall have salvation. Amen.

5

LOVE'S CROWNING DEED

"Greater love has no man than this,
that a man lay down his life for his friends."
—John 15:13

I have lately in my ministry very much detained you in the balmy region of divine lovingkindness. Our subjects have frequently been full of love. I have, perhaps, repeated myself, and gone over the same ground again and again, but I could not help it. My own soul was in a grateful condition, and therefore out of the abundance of the heart the mouth has spoken. (See Matthew 12:34.) Truly I have little reason to excuse myself, for the region of love to Christ is the native place of the Christian. We were first brought to know Christ and to rest in Him through His love, and there, in the warmth of His tenderness, we were born to God. Not by the terrors of justice nor the threats of vengeance were we reconciled, but divine grace drew us with cords of love.

Now, we have sometimes heard of sickly persons, that the physician has recommended them to try their native air, in hopes of restoration. So we, also, recommend every backsliding Christian to try the native air of Christ's love, and we charge every healthy believer to abide in it. Let the believer under decays of grace go back to the cross—there he found his hope; there he must find it again. There his love to Jesus began—*"We love Him, because He first loved us"* (1 John 4:19)—and there must His love be again inflamed. The atmosphere around the cross of Christ is bracing to the soul. Get to think much of His love, and you grow strong and vigorous in grace.

As the dwellers in the low-lying Alpine valleys become weak and full of disease in the close, damp atmosphere, but soon recover health and strength if they climb the hillside and tarry there, so in this world of selfishness, where every man is fighting for his own, and the mean spirit of caring only for one's own self reigns predominant, the saints become weak and diseased, even as worldlings are. But up on the hillsides, where we learn Christ's self-denying, disinterested affection to the sons of men, we are braced to nobler and better lives. If men are ever to be truly great, they must be nurtured beneath the wing of free grace and dying love.

The grandeur of the Redeemer's example suggests to His disciples to make their own lives sublime and furnishes them with both motives for doing so and forces to constrain them thereto. Moreover, we may well tarry for many a day in the region of the love of Christ, because not only is it our native region and full of bracing influences, but it has an outlook toward the better shore. As shipwrecked mariners upon a desert island have been known to linger most of the day upon that headland which pushes farthest out into the main ocean, in the hope that, perhaps, if they cannot catch a glimpse of their own country across the waves, they may possibly discern a sail which had left one of the ports of the well-beloved land, so it is that while we are sitting on the headlands of divine love we may look across to heaven and become familiar with the spirits of the just.

If ever we are to see heaven while we are yet tarrying here, it must surely be from Cape Cross or Mount Fellowship—from that jutting piece of holy experience of divine love which runs away from the ordinary thoughts of men and approaches the heart of Christ. There, at any rate, do I long to sit for many an hour, till the eternal day shall break and the shadows flee away. And I shall dwell with all the chosen in the land where there is no more sin—for if there can be found a heaven below, it is where heaven came down from heaven to die for sinful men, that sinful men might go up to heaven to live eternally.

Our subject this morning, then, is divine love, and we have chosen the highest hill in all the goodly land for you to climb. We shall take you today to love's most sacred shrine, to the Jerusalem of the holy land of love, to the labor of love where it was transfigured and put on its most beautiful garments—where it became, indeed, too bright for mortal eye fully to gaze upon it, too lustrous for this dim vision of ours. Let us come to Calvary, where we find love stronger than death, conquering the grave for our sakes!

We shall speak first upon love's crowning act: *"Greater love has no man than this, that a man lay down his life for his friends"* (John 15:13). But then, since the text, grand as it is, and high—so that we cannot attain unto it (see Psalm 139:6)—yet seems to fall short of the great argument, though it is one of the Master's own sayings, we shall speak upon the sevenfold crown of Jesus's love. And when we have done so, we shall have some royal things to say which befit the place whereon we stand when we are gathered at the foot of the cross.

I. LOVE'S CROWNING DEED

There is a climax to everything, and the climax of love is to die for a beloved one. "Free grace and dying love" are the noblest themes among men, and, when united, they are sublimity itself. Love can do much, can do infinite things, but greater love has no man than this, that he lay down his life for his friends. This is the *ultima Thule* of love—its sails can find no further shore; its deeds of self-denial can go no further. To lay down one's life is the most that love can do. This is clear if we consider, first, that when a man dies for his friends, it proves his deep sincerity. Lip-love, proverbially, is a thing to be questioned—too often is it a counterfeit. Love which speaks can use hyperbolical expressions at its will, but when you have heard all you can hear of love's speech, you are not sure that it is love, for all are not hunters that blow the horn; all are not friends who cry up friendship.

There is much among men of a feeling which bears all the likeness of that priceless thing called love, which is more precious than the gold of Ophir; and yet, for all that, as all is not gold that glitters, so it is not all love that walks delicately and feigns affection. But a man is no liar when he is willing to die to prove his love. All suspicion of insincerity must then be banished. We are sure he loves who dies for love. Yes, it is not bare sincerity that we see in such a case—we see the intensity of his affection.

A man may make us feel that he is intensely in earnest when he speaks with burning words, and he may perform many actions which may all appear to show how intense he is; and yet, for all that, he may be but a skillful player, understanding well the art of simulating that which he does not feel. But when a man dies for the cause he has espoused, you know that his is no superficial passion! You are sure that the core of his nature must be on fire when his love consumes his life. If he will shed his blood for the object loved, there must be blood in the veins of his love—it is a living love. Who can question the solemn vehemence of a man's love when he passes through the sepulcher and yields his soul up for the thing he professes to love? So that *"greater love has no man than this"* (John 15:13), because he can give no greater proof of the sincerity and intensity of his affection than to lay down his life for his friends.

And, again, it proves the thorough self-abnegation of the heart when the man risks life itself for love. Love and self-denial for the object loved go hand in hand. If I profess to love a certain person and yet will neither give my silver nor my gold to relieve his needs, nor in any way deny myself comfort or ease for his sake, such love is contemptible. It wears the name but lacks the reality of love. True love must be measured by the degree to which the person loving will be willing to subject himself to crosses and losses, to suffering and self-denials. After all, the value of a thing in the market is what a man will give for it, and you must estimate the value of a man's love by that which he is willing to give up for it. What will he do to prove his affection? What will he suffer for the sake of benefiting his beloved? Greater love for friends has no man than this, that he lay down his life for them.

Even Satan acknowledged the reality of the virtue which would lead a man to die, when he spoke concerning Job to God. He made little of Job's losing his sheep, and his cattle, and his children, and remaining patient. But he said, "*Skin for skin, yea, all that a man has will he give for his life. But put forth Your hand now, and touch his bone and his flesh, and he will curse You to Your face*" (Job 2:4–5). So, if love could give up its cattle and its land, its outward treasures and possessions, it would be somewhat strong, but comparatively it would fail if it could not go further and endure personal suffering—yes, and the laying down of life itself.

No such failure occurred in the Redeemer's love. Our Savior stripped Himself of all His glories and by a thousand self-denials proved His love. But the most convincing evidence was given when He gave up His life for us. "*Hereby perceive we the love of God,*" says the apostle John, "*because He laid down His life for us*" (1 John 3:16). As if John passed by everything else which the Son of God had done for us and put his finger upon His death and said, "Hereby we perceive the love of God toward us." It was majestic love that made the Lord Jesus lay aside "His attire and rings of light," and lend their glory to the stars. He stripped off His azure mantle and hung it on the sky and then came down to earth to wear the poor, mean garments of our flesh and blood—in which to toil and labor like ourselves. But the masterpiece of love was when He would even put off the garment of His flesh and yield Himself to the superlative agonies of death by crucifixion! He could go no further. Self-abnegation had achieved its utmost. He could deny Himself no more when He denied Himself leave to live.

Again, beloved, the reason why death for its object is the crowning deed of love is this, that it excels all other deeds. Jesus Christ had proven His love by dwelling among His people as their Brother and participating in their poverty as their Friend, till He could say, *"The foxes have holes, and the birds of the air have nests; but the Son of Man has not where to lay His head"* (Matthew 8:20). He had manifested His love by telling them all He knew of the Father, unveiling the secrets of eternity to simple fishermen. He showed His love by the patience with which He bore with their faults, never harshly rebuking but only gently chiding them—and even that but seldom. He revealed His love to them by the miracles He worked on their behalf and the honor which He put upon them by using them in His service. Indeed, there were ten thousand princely acts of the love of Jesus Christ toward His own, but none of them can for a moment endure comparison with His dying for them—the agonizing death of the cross surpasses all the rest!

These life-actions of His love are bright as stars, and, like the stars, if you gaze upon them, they will be seen to be far greater than you dreamed, but yet they are only stars compared with this clear, blazing sun of infinite love which is to be seen in the Lord's dying for His people on the bloody tree. Then, I must add that His death did, in effect, comprehend all other acts, for when a man lays down his life for his friend, he has laid down everything else. Give up life, and you have given up wealth—where is the wealth of a dead man? Renounce life, and you have relinquished position— where is the rank of a man who lies in the sepulcher? Lay down life, and you have forsaken enjoyment—what enjoyment can there be to the denizen of the morgue? Giving up life, you have given up all things, hence the force of that reasoning, *"He that spared not His own Son, but delivered Him up for us all, how shall He not with Him also freely give us all things?"* (Romans 8:32).

The giving of the life of His dear Son was the giving of all that His Son was. And, as Christ is infinite and all in all, the delivering up of His life was the concession of all in all to us—there could be nothing more. Beloved, I speak but too coldly upon a theme which ought to stir my soul first and yours afterward. Spirit of the living God, come like a quickening wind from heaven and let the sparks of our love glow into a mighty furnace just now, even now, if it may so please You! Beloved, we now remark that for a man to die for his friends is evidently the grandest of all proofs of his love in itself. The words glide over my tongue and drop from my lips very readily—*"lay down his life for his friends"*—but do you know or feel what the words mean?

To die for another! There are some who will not even give of their substance to the poor. It seems like wrenching away a limb for them to give a trifle to God's poor servants. Such people cannot guess what it must be to have love enough to die for another, any more than a blind man can imagine what colors can be like—such persons are out of court altogether. There have been loving spirits who have denied themselves comfort and ease, and even common necessities, for the sake of their fellow men. Only such as these are in a measure qualified to form an idea of what it must be to die for another. But still, none of us can fully know what it means. To die for another! Conceive it! Concentrate your thoughts upon it! We start back from death, for under any light in which you may place it, human nature can never regard death as otherwise than a terrible thing.

To pass away into the glory-land is so bright a hope that death is swallowed up in the victory (see 1 Corinthians 15:54), but the death itself is a bitter thing and therefore needs to be swallowed up in the victory before we can bear it. It is a bitter pill and must be drowned in a sweet potion before we can rejoice in it. I am certain that no person, apart from sweet reflections of the presence of God and the heavenly future, could regard death other than as a dreadful calamity. Even our Savior did not regard His approaching death without trembling! The thought of dying was not, in itself, otherwise than saddening, even to Him. Witness the bloody sweat as it streamed from Him in Gethsemane, and that manlike putting away of the cup with, "*If it is possible, let this cup pass from Me*" (Matthew 26:39)!

As you think of that soul-conflict, let it increase your idea of the Godlike love which took the cup resolutely, with both its hands, drank right on, and never stayed its dreadful draught till the Lord had drunk damnation dry for all His people, swallowing up their deaths in His own most comprehensive death! It is no light thing to die. We speak too flippantly of death, but dying is no child's play to any man—and dying as the Savior died, in awful agonies of body and tortures of soul, it was a great thing, indeed, for His love to do. You may surround death, if you please, with luxury. You may place at the bedside all the dear assuagements of the most tender love. You may alleviate pain by the art of the apothecary and the physician. And you may decorate the dying couch with the honor of a nation's anxious care. But death, for all that, is, in itself, no slight thing—and when borne for others it is the masterpiece of love.

And so, closing this point of love's crowning action, let me say that after a man has died for another, there can be no question raised about his love. Unbelief would be insane if it should venture to intrude itself at the foot of the cross, though, alas, it has been there and has there proved its utter unreasonableness! If a man dies for his friend, he must love him; nobody can question that! And Jesus, dying for His people, must love them—who shall cast a doubt upon that fact? Shame on any of God's children that they should ever raise questions on a matter so conclusively proven! As if the Lord Jesus knew that even this masterpiece of love might still be intruded upon by unbelief, He rose again from the dead and rose with His love as fresh as ever in His heart—and went to heaven leading captivity captive, His eyes flashing with the eternal love that brought Him down!

He passed through the pearly gates and rode in triumph up to His great Father's throne, and though He looked upon His Father with love ineffable and eternal, He gazed upon His people, too, for His heart was still theirs. Even at this hour, from His throne among the seraphim, where He sits in glory, He looks down upon His people with pitying love and condescending grace:

Now, though He reigns exalted high,
His love is still as great:
Well He remembers Calvary,
Nor let His saints forget.

He is all Love and altogether Love. *"Greater love has no man than this, that a man lay down his life for his friends"* (John 15:13).

II. THE SEVEN CROWNS OF JESUS'S DYING LOVE

I hope I shall have your interested attention while I show that above that highest act of human love there is something in Christ's death for love's sake still more elevated. Men's dying for their friends, this is superlative—but Christ's dying for us is as much above man's superlative as that could be above mere commonplace. Let me show you this in seven points.

I. IMMORTALITY MADE JESUS'S DEATH SPECIAL

Jesus is immortal, hence the special character of His death. Damon is willing to die for Pythias. The classic story shows that each of the two friends was anxious to die for the other. But suppose Damon dies for Pythias—he is only antedating what must occur, for Damon must die one day, and if he lays down his life for his friend, say, ten years before he otherwise would have done so, still he only loses that ten years' life—he must die sooner or later. Or if Pythias dies, and Damon escapes, it may be that only by a few weeks one of them has anticipated the departure, for they must both die eventually. When a man lays down his life for his friend, he does not lay down what he could keep altogether. He could only have kept it for a while. Even if he had lived as long as mortals can, till gray hairs are on his head, he must, at last, have yielded to the arrows of death.

A substitutionary death for love's sake in ordinary cases would be but a slightly premature payment of that debt of nature which must be paid by all. But such is not the case with Jesus. Jesus needed not die at all! There was no ground or reason why He should die apart from His laying down His life in the place of His friends. Up there in glory was the Christ of God forever with the Father, eternal and everlasting. No age passed over His brow. We may say of Him, "Your locks are bushy and black as the raven; You have the dew of Your youth." (See Song of Solomon 5:11; Psalm 110:3.) He came to earth and assumed our nature, that He might be capable of death; yet, remember, though capable of death, His body need not have died. As it was, it never saw corruption because there was not in it the element of sin which necessitated death and decay.

Our Lord Jesus, and none but He, could stand at the brink of the grave and say, "*No man takes it from Me, but I lay it down of Myself. I have power to lay it down, and I have power to take it again*" (John 10:18). We poor mortal men have only power to die, but Christ had power to live! Crown Him, then! Set a new crown upon His beloved head! Let other lovers who have died for their friends be crowned with silver, but for Jesus, bring forth the golden diadem and set it upon the head of the Immortal who never needed to have died and yet became a mortal, yielding Himself to death's pangs without necessity, except the necessity of His mighty love!

2. OTHERS WHO LAID DOWN THEIR LIVES HAD A HOPE OF ESCAPING

In the cases of persons who have yielded up their lives for others, they may have entertained and probably did entertain the prospect that the supreme penalty would not be exacted from them. Damon stood before Dionysius, the tyrant, willing to be slain instead of Pythias. But you will remember that the tyrant was so struck with the devotion of the two friends that he did not put either of them to death, and so the proffered substitute escaped. There is an old story of a pious miner who was in the pit with an ungodly man at work. They had lit the fuse and were about to blast a piece of rock with the powder, and it was necessary that they should both leave the mine before the powder exploded.

They both got into the bucket, but the hand above which was to wind them up was not strong enough to draw the two together, and the pious miner, leaping from the bucket, said to his friend, "You are an unconverted man, and if you die your soul will be lost. Get up in the bucket as quickly as you can! As for me, I commit my soul into the hands of God; if I die, I am saved." This lover of his neighbor's soul was spared, for he was found in perfect safety arched over by the fragments which had been blown from the rock—he escaped.

But remember well that such a thing could not occur in the case of our dear Redeemer. He knew that if He was to give a ransom for our souls, He had no loophole for escape. He must surely die. It was either He die, or His people must—there was no other alternative. If we were to escape from the pit through Him, He must perish in the pit Himself. There was no hope for Him. There was no way by which the cup could pass from Him.

Men have bravely risked their lives for their friends. Perhaps, had they been certain that the risk would have ended in death, they would have hesitated. Jesus was certain that our salvation involved death to Him—the cup must be drained to the bottom; He must endure the mortal agony, and in all the extreme sufferings of death, He must not be spared one jot or tittle. Yet deliberately, for our sakes, He espoused death that He might espouse us.

I say again, bring forth another diadem! Put a second crown upon that once thorn-crowned head! All hail, Immanuel! Monarch of Misery and Lord of Love! Was ever love like Yours? Lift up His praises, all you sons of song! Exalt Him, all you heavenly ones! Yes, set His throne higher than the stars! And let Him be extolled above the angels, because with full intent He bowed His head to death. He knew that it behooved Him to suffer, it behooved that He should be made a sacrifice for sin, and yet for the joy that was set before Him, He endured the cross, despising its shame. (See Hebrews 12:2.)

3. JESUS'S MOTIVES WERE PURE

A third grand excellency in the crowning deed of Jesus's love is that He could have had no motive in that death but one of pure, unmingled love and pity. You remember when the Russian nobleman was crossing the steppes of that vast country in the snow, the wolves followed the sledge in greedy packs, eager to devour the travelers. The horses were lashed to their utmost speed but needed not the lash, for they fled for their lives from their howling pursuers. Whatever could stay the eager wolves for a time was thrown to them in vain. A horse was loosed—they pursued it, tore it to pieces, and still followed, like grim death. At last, a devoted servant, who had long lived with his master's family, said, "There remains but one hope for you. I will throw myself to the wolves, and then you will have time to escape."

There was great love in this, but doubtless it was mingled with a habit of obedience, a sense of reverence to the head of the household, and probably emotions of gratitude for many obligations which had been received through a long course of years. I do not depreciate the sacrifice—far from it. Would that there were more of such a noble spirit among the sons of men! But still, you can see a wide difference between that noble sacrifice and the nobler deed of Jesus laying down His life for those who never obliged Him, never served Him—who were infinitely His inferiors and who could have no claims upon His gratitude.

If I had seen the nobleman surrender himself to the wolves to save his servant, and if that servant had in former days tried to be an assassin and had sought his life—and yet the master had given himself up for the undeserving menial—I could see some parallel. But, as the case stands, there is a wide distinction.

Jesus had no motive in His heart but that He loved us—loved us with all the greatness of His glorious nature—loved us, and therefore for love, pure love, and love alone, gave Himself up to bleed and die...

> With all His sufferings full in view,
> And woes to us unknown,
> Forth to the task His spirit flew,
> 'Twas love that urged Him on.

Put the third crown upon His glorious head! O angels, bring forth the immortal coronet which has been stored up for ages for Him alone, and let it glitter upon that ever-blessed brow!

4. JESUS'S DEATH WAS NOT FOR THE SAKE OF HIS FRIENDS ALONE

In our Savior's case, it was not precisely, though it was, in a sense, death for His friends. Greater love has no man than this toward his friends that he lay down his life for them. (See John 15:13.) Read the text so, and it expresses a great truth—but greater love a man may have than to lay down his life for his friends, namely, if he dies for his enemies! And here is the greatness of Jesus's love, that though He called us "friends" (see John 15:15), the friendship was all on His side at the first. He called us friends, but our hearts called Him enemy, for we were opposed to Him. We loved not in return for His love. *"We hid as it were our faces from Him; He was despised, and we esteemed Him not"* (Isaiah 53:3).

Oh, the enmity of the human heart to Jesus! There is nothing like it! Of all enmities that have ever come from the pit that is bottomless, the enmity of the heart to the Christ of God is the strangest and most bitter of all! And yet for men polluted and depraved, for men hardened till their hearts are like the nether millstone, for men who could not return and could not reciprocate the love He felt, Jesus Christ gave Himself to die! *"Scarcely for a righteous man will one die: yet perhaps for a good man some would even dare to die. But God commends His love toward us, in that, while we were yet sinners, Christ died for us"* (Romans 5:7–8).

> O love of unexampled kind!
> That leaves all thought so far behind;
> Where length, and breadth, and depth, and height,
> Are lost to my astonished sight.

Bring forth the royal diadem again, I say, and crown our loving Lord, the Lord of Love, for as He is King of kings everywhere else, so is He King of kings in the region of affection!

5. WE WERE THE REASON A DEATH WAS REQUIRED

Another glorious point about Christ's dying for us is that we had ourselves been the cause of the difficulty which required a death. There were two brothers on board a raft once, upon which they had escaped from a foundering ship. There was not enough food, and it was proposed to reduce the number that some, at least, might be able to live. So many must die. They cast lots for life and death. One of the brothers was drawn and was doomed to be thrown into the sea. His brother interposed and said, "You have a wife and children at home. I am single and therefore can be better spared. I will die instead of you." "No," said his brother, "not so. Why should you? The lot has fallen upon me." And they struggled with each other in mutual arguments of love, till at last the substitute was thrown into the sea.

Now, there was no ground of difference between those two brothers whatever. They were friends, and more than friends. They had not caused the difficulty which required the sacrifice of one of them. They could not blame one another for forcing upon them the dreadful alternative. But in our case, there would never have been a need for anyone to die if we had not been the offenders, the willful offenders. And who was the offended One? Whose injured honor required the death? I speak not untruthfully if I say it was the Christ that died who was, Himself, the offended One. Against God the sin had been committed, against the majesty of the divine Ruler! And in order to wipe the stain away from divine justice, it was imperative that the penalty should be exacted and the sinful one should die. So, He who was offended took the place of the offender and died, that the debt due to His own justice might be paid. It is the case of the judge bearing the penalty which he feels compelled to pronounce upon the culprit!

Like the old classic story of the father who, on the judgment bench, condemns his son to lose his eyes for an act of adultery, and then puts out one of his own eyes to save an eye for his son—the judge himself bore a portion of the penalty. In our case, He who vindicated the honor of His own law and bore all the penalty was the Christ who loved those who had offended His sovereignty and grieved His holiness! I say again—but where are the lips that shall say it aright?—bring forth, bring forth a new diadem of more than imperial splendor to crown the Redeemer's blessed head anew, and let all the harps of heaven pour forth the richest music in praise of His supreme love!

6. MEN WHO HAVE DIED FOR OTHERS DID NOT BEAR THEIR SIN AND GUILT

There have been men who have died for others, but they have never borne the sins of others; They were willing to take the punishment but not the guilt. Those cases which I have already mentioned did not involve character. Pythias has offended Dionysius, Damon is ready to die for him, but Damon does not bear the offense given by Pythias. A brother is thrown into the sea for a brother, but there is no fault in the case. The servant dies for his master in Russia, but the servant's character rises—it is in no degree associated with any fault of the master—and the master is, indeed, faultless in the case. But here, before Christ must die, it must be written, *"He was numbered with the transgressors; and He bore the sin of many"* (Isaiah 53:12). *"The LORD has laid on Him the iniquity of us all"* (Isaiah 53:6). *"He has made Him to be sin for us, who knew no sin; that we might be made the righteousness of God in Him"* (2 Corinthians 5:21). He was *"made a curse for us: for it is written, Cursed is every one that hangs on a tree"* (Galatians 3:13).

Now, far be it from our hearts to say that Christ was ever less than perfectly holy and spotless, and yet there had to be established a connection between Him and sinners by the way of substitution, which must have been hard for His perfect nature to endure. For Him to be hung up between two felons (see Matthew 27:38), for Him to be accused of blasphemy (see Matthew 26:65), for Him to be numbered with transgressors (see Luke 22:37), for Him to suffer, the Just for the unjust (see 1 Peter 3:18), bearing His Father's wrath as if He had been guilty—this is amazing and surpasses all thought! Bring forth the brightest crowns and put them on His head, while we pass on to weave a seventh chaplet for that laudable brow!

7. CHRIST HAD NO COMFORT IN HIS DEATH

The death of Christ was a proof of superlative love, because in His case He was denied all the helps and alleviations which in other cases make death to be less than death. I marvel not that a saint can die joyously. Well may his brow be placid and his eyes bright, for he sees his heavenly Father gazing down upon him and glory awaiting him! Well may his spirit be rapt in joy, even while the death-sweat is on his face, for the angels have come to meet him, and he sees the far-off land and the gates of pearl growing nearer every hour! But, ah, to die upon a cross without a pitying eye upon you, surrounded by a scoffing multitude—and to die there appealing to God, who turns away His face! To die with this as your requiem: *"My God, My God, why have You forsaken Me?"* (Matthew 27:46). To startle the midnight darkness with *"Eli, Eli, lama sabachthani?"* (Matthew 27:46)—a cry of awful anguish such as never had been heard before—this is terrible!

The triumph of love in the death of Jesus rises clear above all other heroic acts of self-sacrifice. Even as we have seen the lone peak of the monarch of mountains rise out from all adjoining alps and pierce the clouds to hold familiar converse with the stars, so does this love of Christ soar far above anything else in human history or that can be conceived by the heart of man! His death was more terrible, His passing away more grievous by far. Greater love has no man than this, that He lay down such a life in such a fashion, and for such enemies so utterly unworthy! Oh, I will not say, "Crown Him"—what are crowns to Him? Blessed Lamb of God, our hearts love You! We fall at Your feet in adoring reverence and magnify You in the silence of our souls.

III. MANY ROYAL THINGS OUGHT TO BE SUGGESTED TO US BY THIS ROYAL LOVE

First, dear brothers and sisters, how this thought of Christ's proving His love by His death ennobles self-denial. I do not know how you feel, but I feel utterly mean when I think of what Christ has done for me. To live a life of comparative ease and enjoyment shames me. To work to weariness seems nothing. After all, what are we doing compared with what He has done? Those who can suffer, who can lay down their lives in mission fields and bear hardships, and poverty, and persecution for Christ—my brethren, these are to be envied—they have a portion above their brethren!

It makes us feel ashamed to be at home and to possess any comforts when Jesus so denied Himself. I say the thought of the Lord's bleeding love makes us think ourselves mean to be what we are. It makes us nothing in our own sight, while it causes us to honor before God the self-denial of others and wish that we had the means of practicing it. And, oh, how it prompts us to hero-ism! When you get to the cross, you have left the realm of little men—you have reached the nursery of true chivalry. Does Christ die?—then we feel we could die, too! What grand things men have done when they have lived in the love of Christ!

That story of the Moravians comes to my mind, and I will repeat it, though you may often have heard it, how, in the South of Africa, there was years ago a place of lepers into which persons afflicted with leprosy were driven. There was a tract of country surrounded by high walls from which none could escape. There was only one gate, and he who went in never came out again. Certain Moravians looked over the wall and saw two men—one whose arms had rotted off with leprosy was carrying on his back another who had lost his legs—and between the two they were making holes in the ground and planting seeds. The two Moravians thought, "They are dying of a foul disease by hundreds inside that place. We will go and preach the gospel to them. But," they said, "if we go in, we can never come out again. There we will die of leprosy, too." They went in, and they never did come out till they went home to heaven. They died for others for the love of Jesus.

Two others of these holy men went to the West Indian Islands, where there was an estate to which a man could not go to preach the gospel unless he was a slave. And these two men sold themselves for slaves, to work as others worked, that they might tell their fellow slaves the gospel. Oh, if we had that spirit of Jesus among us, we should do great things! We need it badly and must have it. The church has lost everything when she has lost her old heroism! She has lost her power to conquer the world when the love of Christ no longer constrains her. But mark how the heroics in this case are sweetly tinctured and flavored with gentleness. The chivalry of the olden times was cruel. It consisted very much in a strong fellow cased in steel going about and knocking others to pieces who did not happen to wear similar suits of steel.

Nowadays we could get a good deal of that courage back, I daresay, but we shall be best without it. We need that blessed chivalry of love in which a man feels, "I would suffer any insult from that man if I could do him good for Christ's sake. And I would be a doormat to my Lord's temple gate, that all who come by might wipe their feet upon me, if they could thereby honor Christ." The grand heroism of being nothing for Christ's sake, or anything for the church's sake—that is the heroism of the cross, for Christ *"made Himself of no reputation, and took upon Him the form of a servant, and was made in the likeness of men: and being found in fashion as a man, He humbled Himself, and became obedient to death, even the death of the cross"* (Philippians 2:7–8). O blessed Spirit, teach us to perform heroic acts of self-abnegation for Jesus's name's sake!

And, lastly, there seems to come to my ears from the cross a gentle voice that says, "Sinner, sinner, guilty sinner, I did all this for you, what have you done for Me?" And yet another which says, "Return unto Me! *Look to Me, and be you saved, all the ends of the earth'* (Isaiah 45:22)." I wish I knew how to preach to you Christ crucified. I feel ashamed of myself that I cannot do better than I have done. I pray the Lord to set it before you in a far better way than any of my words can. But, oh, guilty sinner, there is life in a look at the Redeemer! Turn now your eyes to Him and trust Him! Simply by trusting Him you shall find pardon, mercy, eternal life, and heaven. Faith is a look at the Great Substitute. God help you to get that look, for Jesus's sake. Amen.

6

THE CROWN OF THORNS

"And when they had platted a crown of thorns,
they put it upon His head."
—Matthew 27:29

Before we enter the common hall of the soldiers and gaze upon "the sacred head once wounded," it will be well to consider who and what He was who was thus cruelly put to shame. Forget not the intrinsic excellence of His person, for He is the brightness of the Father's glory and the express image of His person. (See Hebrews 1:3.) He is in Himself God over all, blessed forever, the eternal Word by whom all things were made and by whom all things consist. (See Colossians 1:16–17.) Though Heir of all things, the Prince of the kings of the earth, He was despised and rejected of men, *"a man of sorrows, and acquainted with grief"* (Isaiah 53:3). His head was scornfully surrounded with thorns for a crown. His body was bedecked with a faded purple robe. A poor reed was put into His hand for a scepter, and then the ribald soldiers dared to spit upon His face and worry Him with their filthy jests (see Matthew 27:27–31):

The soldiers also spit upon that face
Which angels did desire to have the grace,
And Prophets once to see, but found no place.
Was ever grief like Mine?

Forget not the glory to which He had been accustomed, for before He came to earth, He had been in the bosom of the Father, adored of cherubim and seraphim, obeyed by every angel, worshipped by every principality and power in the heavenly places! Yet here He sits, treated worse than a felon, made the center of a comedy before He became the victim of a tragedy. They sat Him down in some broken chair, covered Him with an old soldier's cloak, and then insulted Him as a mimic monarch:

They bow their knees to Me, and cry, Hail king:
Whatever scoffs and scornfulness can bring,
I am the floor, the sink, where they'd fling.
Was ever grief like Mine?

What a descent His love for us compelled Him to make! See how He fell to lift us from our fall! Do not also fail to remember that at the very time when they were thus mocking Him, He was still the Lord of All and could have summoned twelve legions of angels to His rescue. (See Matthew 26:53.) There was majesty in His misery! He had laid aside, it is true, the glorious, imperial pomp of His Father's courts, and He was now the lowly Man of Nazareth; but for all that, had He willed it, one glance of those eyes would have withered up the Roman cohorts. One word from those silent lips would have shaken Pilate's palace from roof to foundation. And, had He willed it, the vacillating governor and the malicious crowd would together have gone down alive into the pit, even as Korah, Dathan, and Abiram of old! (See Numbers 16.)

Lo, God's own Son, heaven's Darling and earth's Prince, sits there and wears the cruel chaplet which wounds both mind and body at once—the mind with insult and the body with piercing pain! His royal face was marred with "wounds which could not cease to bleed, trickling faint and slow." Yet that "noblest brow and dearest head" had once been fairer than the children of men and was even then the countenance of Immanuel, God with us! Remember these things, and you will gaze upon Him with enlightened eyes and tender hearts—and you will be able, the more fully, to enter into fellowship with Him in His griefs. Remember from where He came, and it will the more astound you that He should have stooped so low! Remember what He was, and it will be the more marvelous that He should become our substitute.

And now let us press into the guardroom and look at our Savior wearing His crown of thorns. I will not detain you long with any guesses as to what kind of thorns He wore. According to the rabbis and the botanists, there would seem to have been from twenty to twenty-five different species of thorny plants growing in Palestine; and different writers have, according to their own judgments or fancies, selected one and another of these plants as the peculiar thorns which were used upon this occasion. But why select one thorn out of many? He bore not one grief but all—any and every thorn will suffice. The very dubiousness as to the peculiar species yields us instruction.

It may well be that more than one kind of thorn was platted in that crown. At any rate, sin has so thickly strewn the earth with thorns and thistles that there was no difficulty in finding the materials, even as there was no scarcity of griefs with which to chasten Him every morning and make Him a mourner all His days. The soldiers may have used pliant boughs of the acacia, or shittim, tree—that unrotting wood of which many of the sacred tables and vessels of the sanctuary were made, and therefore significantly used, if such were the case. It may have been true, as the old writers generally consider, that the plant was the spina-christi, for it has many small and sharp spines. And its green leaves would have made a wreath such as those with which generals and emperors were crowned after a battle.

But we will leave the matter. It was a crown of thorns which pierced His head and caused Him suffering as well as shame—and that suffices us. Our inquiry now is, what do we see when our eyes behold Jesus Christ crowned with thorns? There are six things which strike me most. And as I lift the curtain, I pray you watch with me, and may the Holy Spirit pour forth His divine illumination and light up the scene before our wondering souls.

I. WE SEE A SORROWFUL SPECTACLE

Here is the Christ, the generous, loving, tender Christ, treated with indignity and scorn! Here is the Prince of Life and Glory made an object of derision by ribald soldiers! Behold today the lily among thorns, purity itself, in the midst of opposing sin! See here the sacrifice caught in the thicket and held fast there, as a victim in our place, to fulfill the ancient type of the ram held by the bushes which Abraham slew instead of Isaac! (See Genesis 22:13.)

Three things are to be carefully noted in this spectacle of sorrow.

1. THE SOLDIERS' TREATMENT OF HIM

Here are Christ's lowliness and weakness triumphed over by the lusty soldiers. When they brought Jesus into the guardroom, they felt that He was entirely in their power and that His claims to be a king were so absurd as to be only a theme for contemptuous jest. He was but meanly dressed, for He wore only the smock frock of a peasant—was He a claimant of the purple? He held His peace—was He the man to stir a nation to sedition? He was all wounds and bruises, fresh from the scourger's lash—was He the hero to inspire an army's enthusiasm and overturn old Rome?

It seemed rare mirth for them, and as wild beasts sport with their victims, so did they. Many, I warrant you, were the jibes and jeers of the Roman soldiers at His expense, and loud was the laughter amid their ranks. Look at His face, how meek He appears! How different from the haughty countenances of tyrants! To mock His royal claims seemed but natural to rough soldiers. He was gentle as a child, tender as a woman! His dignity was that of calm quiet endurance—and this was not a dignity whose force these semi-barbarous men could feel, and therefore they did pour contempt upon Him. Let us remember that our Lord's weakness was undertaken for our sakes: for us He became a lamb; for us He laid aside His glory. And therefore it is the more painful for us to see that this voluntary humiliation of Himself must be made the object of so much derision and scorn, though worthy of the utmost praise.

He stoops to save us, and we laugh at Him as He stoops! He leaves the throne that He may lift us up to it, but while He is graciously descending, the hoarse laughter of an ungodly world is His only reward! Ah, me, was ever love treated after so unlovely a sort? Surely the cruelty it received was proportioned to the honor it deserved, so perverse are the sons of men:

> O head so full of bruises!
> Brow that its lifeblood loses!
> Oh great humility.
> Upon His face are falling
> Indignities most galling;
> He bears them all for me.

2. THE SOLDIERS' MOCKING OF HIS CLAIMS

It was not merely that the soldiers mocked His humility; they also mocked His claims to be a king. "Aha," they seemed to say, "is this a king? It must be after some uncouth Jewish fashion, surely, that this poor Peasant claims to wear a crown. Is this the Son of David? When will He drive Caesar and his armies into the sea and set up a new state, and reign at Rome? This Jew, this Peasant—is He to fulfill His nation's dream and rule over all mankind?" In wonderment did they ridicule this idea, and we do not wonder that they did, for they could not perceive His true glory.

But, beloved, my point lies here: He was a King in the truest and most emphatic sense. If He had not been a King, then He would, as an impostor, have deserved the scorn but would not have keenly felt it. But, with His being truly and really a King, every word must have stung His royal soul, and every syllable must have cut His kingly spirit to the quick. When the impostor's claims are exposed and held up to scorn, he himself must well know that he deserves all the contempt he receives—and what can he say? But if the real Heir to all the estates of heaven and earth has His claims denied and His person mocked, then is His heart wounded, and rebuke and reproach fill Him with many sorrows. Is it not sad that the Son of God, the blessed and only Potentate, should have been thus disgraced?

3. THE SOLDIERS' CRUELTY

The soldiers did not merely mock Jesus; their cruelty added pain to insult. If they had only intended to mock Him, they might have platted a crown of straw. But they meant to hurt Him, and, therefore, they fashioned a crown of thorns. Look, I pray you, at His person as He suffers under their hands! They had scourged Him till probably there was no part of His body which was not bleeding beneath their blows except His head—and now that head must be made to suffer, too.

Alas, our whole head was sick and our whole heart faint—and so He must be made, in His chastisement, like unto us in our transgression. There was no part of our humanity without sin—and there must be no part of His humanity without suffering. If we had escaped, in some measure, from iniquity, so might He have escaped from pain. But, as we had worn the foul garment of transgression and it covered us from head to foot, even so must He wear the garments of shame and derision from the crown of His head, even to the soles of His feet:

> Love, too boundless to be shown
> By any but the Lord alone!
> O Love offended, which sustains
> The bold offender's curse and pains!
> O Love, which could no motive have,
> But mere benignity to save.

Beloved, I always feel as if my tongue were tied when I come to talk of the sufferings of my Master. I can think of them; I can picture them to myself; I can sit down and weep over them—but I know not how to paint them to others! Did you ever know pen or pencil that could? A Michelangelo or a Raphael might well shrink back from attempting to paint this picture! And the tongue of an archangel might be consumed in the effort to sing the griefs of Him who was loaded with shame because of our shameful transgressions.

I ask you rather to meditate than to listen—and to sit down and view your Lord with your own loving eyes rather than to have regard to any words of mine. I can only sketch the picture, roughly outlining it as with charcoal. I must leave you to put in the colors and then to sit and study it—but you will fail, as I do. Dive as we may, we cannot reach the depths of this abyss of woe and shame! Climb as we may, these storm-swept hills of agony are still above us.

II. WE SEE A SOLEMN WARNING

This warning speaks softly and meltingly to us out of the spectacle of sorrow. Do you ask me what is that warning? It is a warning against our ever committing the same crime as the soldiers did. "The same?" you ask. "Why, we should never plat a crown of thorns for that dear head." I pray you never may. But there are many who have done so and are doing it now! Those are guilty of this crime who, as these soldiers did, deny His claims. Busy are the wise men of this world at this very time all over the world—busy in gathering thorns and twisting them, that they may afflict the Lord's Anointed. Some of them cry, "Yes, He was a good Man, but not the Son of God!" Others even deny His superlative excellence in life and teaching. They quibble at His perfection and imagine flaws where none exist. Never are they happier than when impugning His character. I may be addressing some avowed nonbeliever here, some skeptic as to the Redeemer's person and doctrine—and I charge him with crowning the Christ of God with thorns every time he invents bitter charges against the Lord Jesus and utters railing words against His cause and His people! Your denial of His claims, and especially your ridicule of them, is a repetition of the unhappy scene before us. There are some who ply all their wit and tax their utmost skill for nothing else but to discover discrepancies in the gospel narratives or to conjure up differences between their supposed scientific discoveries and the declarations of the Word of God. Full often have they torn their own hands in weaving crowns of thorns for Him, and I fear, as the result of their displays of scientific research after briers with which to afflict the Lover of mankind, some of them will have to lie upon a bed of thorns when they come to die.

It will be well if they have not to lie on worse than thorns forever when Christ shall come to judge them and condemn them and cast them into the lake of fire for all their impieties concerning Him. Oh, that they would cease this useless and malicious trade of weaving crowns of thorns for Him who is the world's only hope, whose religion is the lone star that gilds the midnight of human sorrow and guides mortal man to the port of peace! Even for the temporal benefits of Christianity the good Jesus should be treated with respect. He has emancipated the slave and uplifted the downtrodden! His gospel is the charter of liberty, the scourge of tyrants, and the death of priests! Spread it, and you spread peace, freedom, order, love, and joy! He is the greatest of philanthropists, the truest Friend of man—why then array yourselves against Him, you who talk of progress and enlightenment? If men did but know Him, they would crown Him with diadems of reverent love more precious than the pearls of India, for His reign will usher in the golden age. Even now it softens the rigor of the present, as it has removed the miseries of the past.

It is an ill business, this carping and quibbling, and I beseech those engaged in it to cease their ungenerous labors, unworthy of rational beings and destructive to their immortal souls!

This crowning with thorns is worked in another fashion by hypocritical professions of allegiance to Him. These soldiers put a crown on Christ's head, but they did not mean that He should be king. They put a scepter in His hand, but it was not the substantial ivory rod which signifies real power—it was only a weak and slender reed. Therein they remind us that Christ is mocked by insincere professors. O you who love Him not in your inmost souls, you are those who mock Him! But you say, "Wherein have I failed to crown Him? Did I not join the church? Have I not said that I am a believer?" Oh, but if your hearts are not right within you, you have only crowned Him with thorns! If you have not given Him your very soul, you have, in awful mockery, thrust a scepter of reed into His hand! Your very religion mocks Him! Your lying professions mock Him!

Who has required this at your hands, to tread His courts? You insult Him at His table! You insult Him on your knees! How can you say you love Him when your hearts are not with Him? If you have never believed in Him and repented of sin, if you have never yielded obedience to His commands, if you do not acknowledge Him in your daily life to be both Lord and King, I charge you, lay down the profession which is so dishonoring to Him! If He is God, serve Him! If He is King, obey Him! If He is neither, then do not profess to be Christians! Be honest and bring no crown if you do not accept Him as King! What need, again, to insult Him with nominal dominion, mimic homage, and pretended service? O you hypocrites! Consider your ways, lest soon the Lord whom you provoke should ease Him of His adversaries!

In a measure the same thing may be done by those who are sincere but, through lack of watchfulness, walk so as to dishonor their profession. Here, if I speak rightly, I shall compel every one of you to confess it in your spirits that you stand condemned—for every time that we act according to our sinful flesh, we crown the Savior's head with thorns. Which of us has not done this? Dear Head, every hair of which is more precious than fine gold, when we gave our hearts to You, we thought we should always adore You! We thought that our whole lives would be one long psalm, praising and blessing and crowning You!

Alas, how far have we fallen short of our own ideals? We have hedged You about with the briers of our sin. We have been betrayed into angry tempers so that we have spoken unadvisedly with our lips. Or we have been worldly and loved that which You abhor, or we have yielded to our passions and indulged our evil desires. Our vanities, follies, forgetfulness, omissions, and offenses have set upon Your head a coronet of dishonor—and we tremble to think of it! Oh, cruel hearts and hands, to have so maltreated the Well-Beloved, whom it should have been our daily care to glorify!

Do I speak to any backslider whose open sin has dishonored the cross of Christ? I fear I must be addressing some who once had a name to live but now are numbered with the dead in sin! Surely, if there is a spark of divine grace in you, what I am now saying must cut you to the quick and act like salt upon a raw wound to make your very soul to smart! Do not your ears tingle as I accuse you of deliberate acts of inconsistency which have twisted a thorny crown for our dear Master's head? It is assuredly so, for you have opened the mouths of blasphemers, taught gainsayers to revile Him, grieved the generation of His people, and made many to stumble. Ungodly men have laid your faults at the door of the innocent Savior—they have said, "This is Your religion."

You have grown the thorns, but He has had to wear them! We call your offenses inconsistencies, but worldly men regard them as the fruit of Christianity and condemn the Vine because of our sour clusters! They charge the holy Jesus with the faults of His erring followers. Dear friends, is there not room to look at home in the case of each one of us? As we do so, let us come with the sorrowful and loving penitent and wash His dear feet with tears of repentance because we have crowned His head with thorns. Thus, our thorn-crowned Lord and Master stands before us as a sorrowful spectacle, conveying to us a solemn warning.

III. WE SEE TRIUMPHANT ENDURANCE

Christ could not be conquered! He was victorious even in the hour of deepest shame—

He with unflinching heart
Bore all disgrace and shame,
And 'mid the keenest smart
Loved on, yes loved the same.

He was bearing, at that moment, first the substitutionary griefs which were due to Him because He stood in our place, and from bearing them He did not turn aside.

We were sinners, and the reward of sin is pain and death—therefore He bore the chastisement of our peace. He was enduring, at that time, what we ought to have endured—and He was draining the cup which justice had mingled for us. Did He start back from it? Oh, no! When He first came to drink of that wormwood and gall in the garden, He put it to His lips, and the draught seemed, for an instant, to stagger even His strong spirit. His soul was exceedingly sorrowful, even unto death. He was like one demented, tossed to and fro with inward agony. *"My Father,"* He said, *"if it be possible, let this cup pass from Me"* (Matthew 26:39). Three times did He utter that prayer, while every portion of His manhood was the battlefield of legions of griefs! His soul rushed out at every pore to find a vent for its swelling woes! His whole body became covered with gory sweat. (See Luke 22:44.)

After that tremendous struggle, the strength of love mastered the weakness of manhood. He put that cup to His lips and never shrank—He drank right on till not a drop was left! And now the cup of wrath is empty—no trace of the terrible wine of the wrath of God can be found within it! At one tremendous draught of love, the Lord drank destruction dry, forever, for all His people. *"Who is he that condemns? It is Christ that died, yea rather, that is risen again"* (Romans 8:34). And *"there is therefore now no condemnation to them which are in Christ Jesus, who walk not after the flesh, but after the Spirit"* (Romans 8:1).

Now, surely, endurance had reached a very high point when our Master was made to endure the painful mockery which our text describes, yet He quailed not, nor removed from His settled purpose. He had undertaken, and He would go through with it. Look at Him and see there a miracle of patient endurance of griefs which would have sent a world to hell had He not borne them on our behalf!

Besides the shame and suffering due for sin, with which it pleased the Father to bruise Him, He was enduring a superfluity of malice from the hate of men. Why did men need to concentrate all their scorn and cruelty into His execution? Was it not enough that He must die? Did it give pleasure to their iron hearts to rack His tender sensibilities? Why these inventions for deepening his woe?

Had any of us been thus derided, we should have resented it. There is not a man or woman here who could have been silent under such indignities! But Jesus sat in omnipotence of patience possessing His soul right royally. Glorious Pattern of patience, we adore You as we see how malice could not conquer Your almighty love! The pain which He had endured from the scourges caused Him to throb with exquisite anguish (see Matthew 27:26)—but we read neither of tears nor groans, much less of angry complaints or revengeful threats. He does not seek pity or make one appeal for leniency. He does not ask why they torture or why they mock. Brave Witness! Courageous Martyr! Suffering exquisitely, You also suffered calmly! Such a perfect frame as His—His body being conceived without sin—He must have been capable of tortures which our bodies, corrupted by sin, cannot feel.

His delicate purity felt a horror of ribald jests which our more hardened spirits cannot estimate. Yet Jesus bore all as only the Son of God could bear it. They might heap on the load as they would— He would only put forth more endurance and bear it all; He would not shrink or complain. I venture to suggest that such was the picture of patience which our blessed Lord exhibited that it may have moved even some of the soldiers themselves. Has it ever occurred to you to ask how Matthew came to know all about that mockery? Matthew was not there! Mark, also, gives an account of it, but he would not have been tolerated in the guardroom. The Praetorians were far too proud and rough to tolerate Jews, much less disciples of Jesus, in their common hall.

Since there could have been nobody there except the soldiers themselves, it is well to inquire: who told this tale? It must have been an eyewitness. May it not have been that centurion who, in the same chapter, is reported to have said, *"Truly this was the Son of God"* (Matthew 27:54)? May not that scene, as well as the Lord's death, have led him to that conclusion?

We do not know, but this much is very evident: the story must have been told by an eyewitness, and also by one who sympathized with the Sufferer, for to my ears it does not read like the description of an unconcerned spectator. I should not wonder—I would almost venture to assert—that our Lord's marred but patient visage preached such a sermon that one, at least, who gazed upon it felt its mysterious power! Certainly at least one felt that such patience was more than human, and accepted the thorn-crowned Savior as his Lord and his King! This I do know, that if you and I want to conquer human hearts for Jesus, we, too, must be patient. And if, when they ridicule and persecute us, we can but endure without repining or retaliation, we shall exercise an influence which even the most brutal will feel—and to which chosen minds will submit themselves.

IV. WE SEE A SACRED MEDICINE

I can only hint at the diseases which the death of the triumphant Sufferer will cure. These blood-sprinkled thorns are plants of renown, precious in heavenly surgery if they are rightly used. Take but a thorn out of this crown and use it as a lancet, and it will let out the hot blood of passion and abate the fever of pride! It is a wonderful remedy for swelling flesh and grievous boils of sin. He who sees Jesus crowned with thorns will loathe to look on self, except it be through tears of contrition. This thorn at the breast will make men sing, but not with notes of self-congratulation— the notes will be those of a dove moaning for her mate.

Gideon taught the men of Succoth with thorns (see Judges 8:15–17), but the lessons were not so salutary as those which we learn from the thorns of Jesus. The sacred medicine which the good Physician brings to us in His thorny crown acts as a tonic and strengthens us to endure, without depression, whatever shame or loss His service may bring upon us.

> Who defeats my fiercest foes?
> Who consoles my saddest woes?
> Who revives my fainting heart,
> Healing all its hidden smart?
> Jesus crowned with thorns.

When you begin to serve God and for His sake endeavor to benefit your fellow mortals, do not expect any reward from men, except to be misunderstood, suspected, and abused. (See 2 Timothy 3:12.) The best men in the world are usually the worst spoken of. An evil world cannot speak well of holy lives. The sweetest fruit is most pecked at by the birds. The mountain nearest heaven is most beaten by the storms—and the loveliest character is the most assailed. Those whom you would save will not thank you for your anxiety but blame you for your interference. If you rebuke their sins, they will frequently resent your warnings. If you invite them to Jesus, they will make light of your entreaties. Are you prepared for this? If not, consider Him who endured such contradiction of sinners against Himself, lest you become weary and faint in your minds. If you succeed in bringing many to Christ, you must not reckon upon universal honor—you will be charged with self-seeking, popularity-hunting, or some such crime—you will be misrepresented, belied, caricatured, and counted as a fool or a knave by the ungodly world. The probabilities are that the crown you will win in this world, if you serve God, will contain more spikes than sapphires, more briers than beryls! When it is put upon your head, pray for divine grace to wear it right gladly, counting it all joy to be like your Lord. (See James 1:2–3.)

Say in your heart, "I feel no dishonor in this dishonor. Men may impute shameful things to me, but I am not ashamed. They may degrade me, but I am not degraded. They may cast contempt upon me, but I am not contemptible." The Master of the house was called Beelzebub and spit upon. They cannot do worse to His household; therefore we scorn their scorn! Thus are we nerved to patience by the patience of the despised Nazarene.

The thorn crown is also a remedy for discontent and affliction. When enduring bodily pain, we are apt to wince and fret, but if we remember Jesus crowned with thorns, we say:

> His way was much rougher and darker than mine;
> Did Christ my Lord suffer, and shall I repine?

And so, our complaints grow dumb—for very shame we dare not compare our maladies with His woes! Resignation is learned at Jesus's feet when we see our great Exemplar made perfect through suffering. The thorn crown is a cure for care. We would cheerfully wear any array which our Lord may prepare for us, but it is a great folly to plat needless thorn crowns for ourselves. Yet I have seen some—who are, I hope, true believers—take much trouble to trouble themselves and labor to increase their own labors. They hasten to be rich; they fret, they toil, they worry, they torment themselves to load themselves with the burden of wealth; they wound themselves to wear the thorny crown of worldly greatness! Many are the ways of making rods for our own backs. I have known mothers make thorn crowns out of their children whom they could not trust with God—they have been worn with family anxieties when they might have rejoiced in God. I have known others make thorn crowns out of silly fears for which there were no grounds whatever, but they seemed ambitious to be fretful, eager to prick themselves with briers. O believer, say to yourself, "My Lord wore my crown of thorns for me! Why should I wear it, too?"

He took our griefs and carried our sorrows that we might be a happy people and be able to obey this command: *"Take therefore no thought for the morrow: for the morrow shall take thought for the things of itself"* (Matthew 6:34). Ours is the crown of lovingkindness and tender mercies—and we wear it when we cast all our cares on Him who cares for us. (See 1 Peter 5:7.) That thorn crown cures us of desire for the vainglories of the world! It dims all human pomp and glory till it turns to smoke! Oh, it takes the glitter from your gold, the luster from your gems, and the beauty from all your dainty gewgaws, to see that no imperial purple can equal the glory of His blood—no gems can rival His thorns! Show and parade cease to attract the soul when once the superlative excellencies of the dying Savior have been discerned by the enlightened eyes!

Who seeks for ease when he has seen the Lord Christ? If Christ wears a crown of thorns, shall we covet a crown of laurel? Why should we desire, like feather-bed soldiers, to have everything arranged for our ease and pleasure? Why this reclining upon couches when Jesus hangs on the cross? Why this soft raiment when He is naked? Why these luxuries when He is treated barbarously? Thus, the crown of thorns cures us, at once, of the vainglory of the world and of our own selfish love of ease. The world's minstrel may cry, "Ho, boy, come here and crown me with rosebuds!" But the pleasure seeker's request is not for us. For us neither delights of the flesh nor the pride of life can have charms while the Man of Sorrows is in view. For us it remains to suffer and to labor till the King shall bid us share His rest.

V. WE SEE A MYSTIC CORONATION

The coronation of Christ with thorns was symbolical and had great meaning in it, for, first, it was to Him a triumphal crown. Christ had fought with sin from the day when He first stood foot to foot with it in the wilderness (see, for example, Matthew 4:1–11) up to the time when He entered Pilate's hall (see John 18:28–40)—and He had conquered it. As a witness that He had gained the victory, behold sin's crown seized as a trophy! What was the crown of sin? Thorns. These sprang from the curse. *"Thorns also and thistles shall it bring forth to you"* (Genesis 3:18) was the coronation of sin—and now Christ has taken away its crown and put it on His own head.

He has spoiled sin of its richest regalia, and He wears it Himself. Glorious Champion, all hail! What if I say that the thorns constituted a mural crown? Paradise was set round with a hedge of thorns so sharp that none could enter it, but our Champion leaped, first, upon the bristling rampart and bore the bloodred banner of His cross into the heart of that better, new Eden which He won for us—never to be lost again. Jesus wears the mural chaplet which denotes that He has opened paradise. It was a wrestler's crown He wore, for He wrestled not with flesh and blood, but with principalities and powers (see Ephesians 6:12)—and He overthrew His foe. It was a racer's crown He wore, for He had run with the mighty and outstripped them in the race. He had well near finished His course and had but a step or two more to take to reach the goal. Here is a marvelous field for enlargement—and we must stop at once, lest we go too far! It was a crown rich with glory despite the shame which was intended by it.

We see in Jesus the Monarch of the realms of misery, the Chief among ten thousand sufferers. Never say, "I am a great sufferer." What are our griefs compared with His? As the poet stood upon the Palatine Mount and thought of Rome's dire ruin, he exclaimed, "What are our woes and sufferings?"[2] Even so, I ask: what are our shallow griefs compared with the infinite sorrows of Immanuel? Well may we "control in our close breasts our petty misery." Jesus is, moreover, the Prince of martyrs. He leads the vanguard among the noble army of suffering witnesses and confessors of the truth of God. Though they died at the stake, or pined in dungeons, or

---

2. George Gordon Byron, "To Rome" from "Childe Harold's Pilgrimage," *The Library of the World's Best Literature. An Anthology in Thirty Volumes*, Charles Dudley Warner (New York: R. S. Peale and J. A. Hill, 1917), https://www.bartleby.com/lit-hub/library/poem/to-rome/.

were cast to wild beasts, none of them claim the first rank. He, the faithful and the true Witness (see Revelation 3:14) with the thorn crown and the cross, stands at the head of them all!

It may never be our lot to join the august band, but if there is an honor for which we might legitimately envy saints of former times, it is this—that they were born in those brave days when the ruby crown was within human grasp and when the supreme sacrifice might have been made! We are cowards, indeed, if in these softer days we are ashamed to confess our Master and are afraid of a little scorn, or tremble at the criticisms of the would-be wise. Rather let us follow the Lamb wherever He goes, content to wear His crown of thorns, that we may, in His kingdom, behold His glory!

VI. WE SEE A MIGHTY STIMULUS

A mighty stimulus to what? Why, first, to fervent love of Him. Can you see Him crowned with thorns and not be drawn to Him? I think that if He could come among us this morning and we could see Him, there would be a loving press around Him to touch the hem of His garment or to kiss His feet. Savior, You are very precious to us! Dearest of all the names above, my Savior and my God, You are always glorious, but in these eyes, You are never more lovely than when arrayed in shameful mockery. The Lily of the Valley and the Rose of Sharon (see Song of Solomon 2:1)—both in one is He, fair in the perfection of His character and bloodred in the greatness of His sufferings. Worship Him! Adore Him! Bless Him! And let your voices sing, "Worthy the Lamb."

This sight is a stimulus, next, to repentance. Did our sins put thorns around His head? Oh, my poor, fallen nature, I will scourge you for scourging Him and make you feel the thorns for causing Him to endure them! What? Can you see your Master put to such shame, and yet hold truce or parley with the sins which pierced Him? It cannot be! Let us declare before God our souls' keen grief that we should make the Savior suffer so! Then let us pray for grace to hedge our lives around with thorns, that from this very day sin may not approach us.

I thought, this day, of how often I have seen the blackthorn growing in the hedge all bristling with a thousand prickles, but right in the center of the bush have I seen the pretty nest of a little bird. Why did the creature place its habitation there? Because the thorns become a protection to it and shelter it from harm. As I meditated last night upon this blessed subject, I thought I would bid you build your nests within the thorns of Christ. It is a safe place for sinners! Neither Satan, sin, nor death can reach you there. Gaze on your Savior's sufferings, and you will see sin atoned for. Fly into His wounds! Fly, you timid, trembling doves! There is no resting place so safe for you! Build your nests, I say again, among these thorns, and when you have done so, and trusted Jesus, and counted Him to be All in all to you, then come and crown His sacred head with other crowns!

What glory does He deserve? What is good enough for Him? If we could take all the precious things from all the treasuries of monarchs, they would not be worthy to be pebbles beneath His feet! If we could bring Him all the scepters, miters, tiaras, diadems, and all other pomp on earth, they would be altogether unworthy to be thrown in the dust before Him! With what shall we crown Him? Come, let us weave our praises together and set our tears for pearls, our love for gold—they will sparkle like so many diamonds in His esteem, for He loves repentance and He loves faith. Let us make a wreath, this morning, with our praises, and crown Him as the Laureate of grace! This day on which He rose from the dead, let us extol Him! Oh, for grace to do it in the heart! And then in the life! And then with the tongue, that we may praise Him forever who bowed His head in shame for us!

7

THE BELIEVING THIEF

*"And he said unto Jesus, LORD, remember me when You
come into Your kingdom. And Jesus said to him, Verily I say
to you, Today shall you be with Me in paradise."*
—Luke 23:42–43

The story of the salvation of the dying thief is a standing instance
of the power of Christ to save and of His abundant willingness to
receive all that come to Him, in whatever plight they may be. I
cannot regard this act of grace as a solitary instance, any more than
the salvation of Zacchaeus (see Luke 19:1–10), the restoration of
Peter (see John 21:15–25), or the call of Saul, the persecutor (see
Acts 9:1–19.) Every conversion is, in a sense, singular: no two are
exactly alike, and yet any one conversion is a type of others. The
case of the dying thief is much more similar to our conversion than
it is dissimilar; in point of fact, his case may be regarded as typical
rather than as an extraordinary incident. So, I shall use it at this
time. May the Holy Spirit speak through it to the encouragement
of those who are ready to despair!

Remember, beloved friends, that our Lord Jesus, at the time
He saved this malefactor, was at His lowest. His glory had been

ebbing out in Gethsemane, and before Caiaphas, and Herod, and Pilate; but it had now reached the utmost low-water mark. Stripped of His garments and nailed to the cross, our Lord was mocked by a ribald crowd and was dying in agony, then was He *"numbered with the transgressors"* (Isaiah 53:12) and made as the offscouring of all things. Yet, while in that condition, He achieved this marvelous deed of grace. Behold the wonder wrought by the Savior when emptied of all His glory and hanged up, a spectacle of shame upon the brink of death! How certain is it that He can do great wonders of mercy now, seeing that He has returned unto His glory and sits upon the throne of light! *"He is able to save them to the uttermost that come to God by Him, seeing He ever lives to make intercession for them"* (Hebrews 7:25). If a dying Savior saved the thief, my argument is that He can do even more now that He lives and reigns. All power is given unto Him in heaven and in earth; can anything at this present time surpass the power of His grace?

It is not only the weakness of our Lord which makes the salvation of the penitent thief memorable; it is the fact that the dying malefactor saw it before his very eyes. Can you put yourself into his place and suppose yourself to be looking upon One who hangs in agony upon a cross? Could you readily believe Him to be the Lord of glory, who would soon come to His kingdom? That was no mean faith which, at such a moment, could believe in Jesus as Lord and King. If the author of Hebrews wanted to add some New Testament examples of remarkable faith to the eleventh of Hebrews, he might certainly commence with this thief, who believed in a crucified, derided, and dying Christ, and cried to Him as to One whose kingdom would surely come. The thief's faith was the more remarkable because he was himself in great pain and bound to die. It is not easy to exercise confidence when you are tortured with deadly anguish. Our own rest of mind has at times been greatly hindered by pain of the body. When we are the subjects of acute suffering, it is not easy to exhibit that faith which we fancy we possess at other times. This man, suffering as he did, and seeing the Savior in so sad a state, nevertheless believed unto life eternal. Herein was such faith as is seldom seen.

Recollect, also, that he was surrounded by scoffers. It is easy to swim with the current and hard to go against the stream. This man heard the priests, in their pride, ridicule the Lord, and the great multitude of the common people, with one consent, joined in the scorning; his comrade caught the spirit of the hour and mocked also (see Luke 23:39), and perhaps he did the same for a while. But through the grace of God he was changed and believed in the Lord Jesus in the teeth of all the scorn. His faith was not affected by his surroundings; but he, dying thief as he was, made sure his confidence. (See Luke 23:42.) Like a jutting rock standing out in the midst of a torrent, he declared the innocence of the Christ whom others blasphemed. (See verse 41.) His faith is worthy of our imitation in its fruits. He had no member that was free except his tongue, and he used that member wisely to rebuke his brother malefactor and defend his Lord. His faith brought forth a brave testimony and a bold confession. I am not going to praise the thief, or his faith, but to extol the glory of that grace divine which gave the thief such faith and then freely saved him by its means. I am anxious to show how glorious is the Savior—that Savior to the uttermost, who, at such a time, could save such a man, and give him so great a faith, and so perfectly and speedily prepare him for eternal bliss. Behold the power of that divine Spirit who could produce such faith on soil so unlikely and in a climate so unpropitious.

Let us enter at once into the center of our sermon. First, *note the man who was our Lord's last companion on earth*; second, *note that this same man was our Lord's first companion at the gate of paradise*; and then, third, let us *note the sermon which our Lord preaches to us from this act of grace*. Oh, for a blessing from the Holy Spirit all the sermon through!

I. THE CRUCIFIED THIEF WAS OUR LORD'S LAST COMPANION ON EARTH

What sorry company our Lord selected when He was here! He did not consort with the religious Pharisees or the philosophic Sadducees, but He was known as *"a friend of publicans and sinners"* (Matthew 11:19). How I rejoice at this! It gives me assurance that He will not refuse to associate with *me*. When the Lord Jesus made a friend of me, He certainly did not make a choice which brought Him credit. Do you think He gained any honor when He made a friend of you? Has He ever gained anything by us? No, my brethren; if Jesus had not stooped very low, He would not have come to me; and if He did not seek the most unworthy, He might not have come to you. You feel it so, and you are thankful that He came *"not to call the righteous, but sinners to repentance"* (Luke 5:32). As the Great Physician, our Lord was much with the sick: He went where there was room for Him to exercise His healing art. The whole have no need of a physician: they cannot appreciate Him nor afford scope for His skill, and therefore He did not frequent their abodes. Yes, after all, our Lord did make a good choice when He saved you and me, for in us He has found abundant room for His mercy and grace. There has been elbow room for His love to work within the awful emptiness of our necessities and sins, and therein He has done great things for us, whereof we are glad.

Lest any here should be despairing, and say, "He will never deign to look on me," I want you to notice that *the last companion of Christ on earth was a sinner, and no ordinary sinner.* He had broken even the laws of man, for he was a robber. One calls him "a brigand"; and I suppose it is likely to have been the case. The brigands of those days mixed murder with their robberies: he was probably a freebooter in arms against the Roman government, making this a pretext for plundering as he had opportunity. At last, he was arrested and was condemned by a Roman tribunal, which, on the whole, was usually just, and in this case was certainly just; for he himself confesses the justice of his condemnation. The malefactor who believed upon the cross was a convict who had lain in the condemned cell and was then undergoing execution for his crimes. A convicted felon was the person with whom our Lord last consorted upon earth. What a lover of the souls of guilty men is He! What a stoop He makes to the very lowest of mankind! To this most unworthy of men the Lord of glory, ere He quitted life, spoke with matchless grace. He spoke to him such wondrous words as never can be excelled if you search the Scriptures through: *"Today shall you be with Me in paradise"* (Luke 23:43). I do not suppose that anywhere in this tabernacle there will be found a man who has been convicted before the law, or who is even chargeable with a crime against common honesty; but if there should be such a person among my hearers, I would invite him to find pardon and change of heart through our Lord Jesus Christ. You may come to Him, whoever you may be; for this man did. Here is a specimen of one who had gone to the extreme of guilt and who acknowledged that he had done so—he made no excuse and sought no cloak for his sin; he was in the hands of justice, confronted with the death-doom—and yet he believed in Jesus and breathed a humble prayer to Him, and he was saved upon the spot. As is the sample, such is the bulk. Jesus saves others of like kind. Let me, therefore, put it very plainly here, that none may mistake me. None of you are excluded from the infinite mercy of Christ, however great your iniquity: if you believe in Jesus, He will save *you*.

This man was not only a sinner; *he was a sinner newly awakened.* I do not suppose that he had seriously thought of the Lord Jesus before. According to the other evangelists, he appears to have joined with his fellow thief in scoffing at Jesus: if he did not actually himself use opprobrious words, he was so far consenting thereunto, that the evangelist did him no injustice when he said, *"The thieves also, which were crucified with Him, cast the same in His teeth"* (Matthew 27:44). Yet, now, on a sudden, he wakes up to the conviction that the man who is dying at his side is something more than a Man. He reads the title over His head and believes it to be true—"This is Jesus the King of the Jews" (Matthew 27:37). Thus believing, he makes his appeal to the Messiah, whom he had so newly found, and commits himself to His hands. My hearer, do you see this truth, that the moment a man knows Jesus to be the Christ of God he may at once put his trust in Him and be saved? A certain preacher, whose gospel was very doubtful, said, "Do you, who have been living in sin for fifty years, believe that you can in a moment be made clean through the blood of Jesus?" I answer, "Yes, we do believe that in one moment, through the precious blood of Jesus, the blackest soul can be made white. We do believe that in a single instant the sins of sixty or seventy years can be absolutely forgiven, and that the old nature, which has gone on growing worse and worse, can receive its death-wound in a moment of time, while the life eternal may be implanted in the soul at once." It was so with this man. He had reached the end of his tether, but, all of a sudden, he woke up to the assured conviction that the Messiah was at his side, and, believing, he looked to Him and lived.

So now, my brothers, if you have never in your life before been the subject of any religious conviction, if you have lived up till now an utterly ungodly life—yet if now you will believe that God's dear Son has come into the world to save men from sin, and will unfeignedly confess your sin and trust in Him, you shall be immediately saved. Ay, while I speak the word, the deed of grace may be accomplished by that glorious One who has gone up into heaven with omnipotent power to save.

I desire to put this case very plainly: *this man, who was the last companion of Christ upon earth, was a sinner in misery.* His sins had found him out: he was now enduring the reward of his deeds. I constantly meet with persons in this condition: they have lived a life of wantonness, excess, and carelessness, and they begin to feel the fire-flakes of the tempest of wrath falling upon their flesh; they dwell in an earthly hell, a prelude of eternal woe. Remorse, like an asp, has stung them, and set their blood on fire: they cannot rest, they are troubled day and night. *"Be sure your sin will find you out"* (Numbers 32:23). It has found them out, and arrested them, and they feel the strong grip of conviction. This man was in that horrible condition: what is more, he was *in extremis*. He could not live long: the crucifixion was sure to be fatal; in a short time, his legs would be broken, to end his wretched existence. He, poor soul, had but a short time to live—only the space between noon and sundown—but it was long enough for the Savior, who is mighty to save. Some are very much afraid that people will put off coming to Christ, if we state this. I cannot help what wicked men do with truth, but I shall state it all the same. If you are now within an hour of death, believe in the Lord Jesus Christ, and you shall be saved. If you never reach your homes again but drop dead on the road, if you will now believe in the Lord Jesus, you shall be saved: saved now, on the spot. As you look to Jesus and trust Him, He will give you a new heart and a right spirit, and will blot out your sins. This is the glory of Christ's grace. How I wish I could extol it in proper language! He was last seen on earth before His death in company with a convicted felon, to whom He spoke most lovingly. Come, O you guilty, and He will receive you graciously!

Once more, *this man whom Christ saved at last was a man who could do no good works.* If salvation had been by good works, he could not have been saved, for he was fastened hand and foot to the tree of doom. It was all over with him as to any act or deed of righteousness. He could say a good word or two, but that was all; he could perform no acts; and if his salvation had depended on an active life of usefulness, certainly he never could have been saved. He was a sinner also who could not exhibit a long-enduring repentance for sin, for he had so short a time to live. He could not have experienced bitter convictions lasting over months and years, for his time was measured by moments, and he was on the borders of the grave. His end was very near, and yet the Savior could save him, and did save him so perfectly, that the sun went not down till he was in paradise with Christ.

This sinner, whom I have painted to you in colors none too black, was *one who believed in Jesus and confessed his faith.* He did trust the Lord. Jesus was a Man, and he called Him so; but he knew that He was also Lord, and he called Him so, and said, *"Lord, remember me"* (Luke 23:42). He had such confidence in Jesus that, if He would but only think of him, if He would only remember him when He came into His kingdom, that would be all that he would ask of Him. Alas, my dear hearers! The trouble about some of you is that you know all about my Lord, and yet you do not trust Him. Trust is the saving act. Years ago, you were on the verge of really trusting Jesus, but you are just as far off from it now as you were then. This man did not hesitate; he grasped the one hope for himself. He did not keep his persuasion of our Lord's Messiahship in his mind as a dry, dead belief, but he turned it into trust and prayer: *"Lord, remember me when You come into Your kingdom"* (Luke 23:42). Oh, that in His infinite mercy many of you would trust my Lord this morning! You shall be saved, I am sure you shall: if you are not saved when you trust, I must myself also renounce all hope. This is all that we have done: we looked, and we lived, and we continue to live, because we look to the living Savior. Oh, that this morning, feeling your sin, you would look to Jesus, trusting Him and confessing that trust! Owning that He is Lord to the glory of God the Father, you must and shall be saved.

In consequence of having this faith which saved him, *this poor man breathed the humble but fitting prayer: "Lord, remember me"* (Luke 23:42). This does not seem to ask much; but, as he understood it, it meant all that an anxious heart could desire. As he thought of the kingdom, he had such clear ideas of the glory of the Savior that he felt that if the Lord would think of him, his eternal state would be safe. Joseph, in prison, asked the chief butler to remember him when he was restored to power; but he forgot him. (See Genesis 40:14, 23.) Our Joseph never forgets a sinner who cried to Him in the low dungeon; in His kingdom He remembers the moanings and groanings of poor sinners who are burdened with a sense of sin. Can you not pray this morning and thus secure a place in the memory of the Lord Jesus?

Thus I have tried to describe the man; and, after having done my best, I shall fail of my object unless I make you see that whatever this thief was, he is a picture of what you are. Especially if you have been a great offender, and if you have been living long without caring for eternal things, you are like that malefactor; and yet you, even you, may do as that thief did: you may believe that Jesus is the Christ, and commit your souls into His hands, and He will save you as surely as He saved the condemned brigand. Jesus graciously says, *"Him that comes to Me I will in no wise cast out"* (John 6:37). This means that if *you* come and trust Him, whoever you may be, He will for no reason, and on no ground, and under no circumstances, ever cast you out. Do you catch that thought? Do you feel that it belongs to you, and that if *you* come to Him, *you* shall find eternal life? I rejoice if you so far perceive the truth.

Few people have so much intercourse with desponding and despairing souls as I have. Poor cast-down ones write to me continually. I scarcely know why. I have no special gift of consolation, but I gladly lay myself out to comfort the distressed, and they seem to know it. What joy I have when I see a despairing one find peace! I have had this joy several times during the week that just ended. How much I desire that any of you who are breaking your hearts because you cannot find forgiveness would come to my Lord, and trust Him, and enter into rest! Has He not said, *"Come to Me, all you that labor and are heavy laden, and I will give you rest"* (Matthew 11:28)? Come and try Him, and that rest shall be yours.

II. THE CRUCIFIED THIEF WAS OUR LORD'S COMPANION AT THE GATE OF PARADISE

I am not going into any speculations as to where our Lord went when He quit the body which hung on the cross. It would seem, from some Scriptures, that He descended into the lower parts of the earth, that He might fill all things. But He very rapidly traversed the regions of the dead. Remember that He died perhaps an hour or two before the thief, and during that time the eternal glory flamed through the underworld and was flashing through the gates of paradise just when the pardoned thief was entering the eternal world. Who is this that enters the pearl-gate at the same moment as the King of glory? Who is this favored companion of the Redeemer? Is it some honored martyr? Is it a faithful apostle? Is it a patriarch, like Abraham, or a prince, like David? It is none of these. Behold, and be amazed at sovereign grace. He that goes in at the gate of paradise with the King of glory is a thief who was saved in the article of death. He is saved in no inferior way and received into bliss in no secondary style. Verily, there are last which shall be first! (See Matthew 20:16.)

Here I would have you notice *the condescension of our Lord's choice.* The comrade of the Lord of glory, for whom the cherub turns aside his sword of fire, is no great one but a newly converted malefactor. And why? I think the Savior took him with Him as a specimen of what He meant to do. He seemed to say to all the heavenly powers, "I bring a sinner with Me; he is a sample of the rest."

Have you never heard of him who dreamed that he stood without the gate of heaven, and while there he heard sweet music from a band of venerable persons who were on their way to glory? They entered the celestial portals, and there was great rejoicing and shouts. Enquiring, "What are these?" he was told that they were the goodly fellowship of the prophets. He sighed and said, "Alas! I am not one of those." He waited a while, and another band of shining ones drew nigh, who also entered heaven with hallelujahs, and when he enquired, "Who are these, and whence came they?" the answer was, "These are the glorious company of the apostles." Again he sighed and said, "I cannot enter with them." Then came another body of men, white-robed and bearing palms in their hands, who marched amid great acclamation into the golden city. These, he learned, were the noble army of martyrs; and again he wept, and said, "I cannot enter with these." In the end he heard the voices of many people and saw a greater multitude advancing, among whom he perceived Rahab and Mary Magdalene, David and Peter, Manasseh and Saul of Tarsus, and he espied especially the thief, who died at the right hand of Jesus. These all entered in—a strange company. Then he eagerly enquired, "Who are these?" and they answered, "This is the host of sinners saved by grace." Then was he exceeding glad, and said, "I can go with these." Yet he thought there would be no shouting at the approach of this company and that they would enter heaven without song; instead of which there seemed to rise a sevenfold hallelujah of praise unto the Lord of love, for there is joy in the presence of the angels of God over sinners that repent. (See Luke 15:10.)

I invite any poor soul here that can neither aspire to serve Christ nor suffer for Him as yet, nevertheless to come in with other believing sinners, in the company of Jesus, who now sets before us an open door.

While we are handling this text, note well *the blessedness of the place* to which the Lord called this penitent. Jesus said, *"Today shall you be with Me in paradise"* (Luke 23:43). Paradise means a garden—a garden filled with delights. The garden of Eden is a type of heaven. We know that paradise means heaven, for the apostle speaks of such a man caught up into paradise, and anon he calls it the third heaven. (See 2 Corinthians 12:1–4.) Our Savior took this dying thief into the paradise of infinite delight, and this is where He will take all of us sinners who believe in Him. If we are trusting Him, we shall ultimately be with Him in paradise.

The next word is better still. Note *the glory of the society* to which this sinner is introduced: *"Today shall you be with Me in paradise"* (Luke 23:43). If the Lord said, *"Today shall you be with Me,"* we should not need Him to add another word; for where He is, is heaven to us. He added the word *"paradise"* because else none could have guessed where He was going. Think of it, you uncomely soul: you are to dwell with the altogether lovely One forever. You poor and needy ones, you are to be with Him in his glory, in His bliss, in His perfection. Where He is, and as He is, you shall be. The Lord looks into those weeping eyes of yours this morning, and He says, "Poor sinner, you shall one day be with Me." I think I hear you say, "Lord, that is bliss too great for such a sinner as I am"; but He replies, *"'I have loved you with an everlasting love: therefore with lovingkindness have I drawn you'* (Jeremiah 31:3), till you shall be with Me where I am."

The stress of the text lies in *the speediness of all this.* *"Verily I say to you, Today shall you be with Me in paradise"* (Luke 23:43). *"Today."* You shall not lie in purgatory for ages, nor sleep in limbo for so many years; but you shall be ready for bliss at once, and at once you shall enjoy it. The sinner was hard by the gates of hell, but almighty mercy lifted him up, and the Lord said, *"Today shall you be with Me in paradise."* What a change from the cross to the crown, from the anguish of Calvary to the glory of the New Jerusalem! In those few hours the beggar was lifted from the dunghill and set among princes. *"Today shall you be with Me in paradise."* Can you measure the change from that sinner, loathsome in his iniquity when the sun was high at noon, to that same sinner clothed in pure white, accepted in the Beloved, in the paradise of God, when the sun went down? O glorious Savior, what marvels You can work! How rapidly can You work them!

Please notice, also, *the majesty of the Lord's grace* in this text. The Savior said to him, "*Verily I say to you, Today shall you be with Me in paradise.*" Our Lord gives His own will as the reason for saving this man: "*I say.*" He says it who claims the right thus to speak. It is He who will have mercy on whom He will have mercy and will have compassion on whom He will have compassion. (See Romans 9:15.) He speaks royally, "*Verily I say to you.*" Are they not imperial words? The Lord is a King in whose word there is power. What He says, none can gainsay. He that hath the keys of hell and of death saith, "*I say unto thee, Today shall you be with Me in paradise.*" Who shall prevent the fulfillment of his word?

Notice *the certainty of it.* He says, "*Verily.*" Our blessed Lord on the cross returned to His old majestic manner, as He painfully turned His head, and looked on His convert. He was wont to begin His preaching with, "*Verily, verily, I say to you*"; and now that He is dying, He uses His favorite manner, and says, "*Verily.*" Our Lord took no oath; His strongest asseveration was, "*Verily, verily.*" To give the penitent the plainest assurance, He says, "*Verily I say to you, Today shall you be with Me in paradise.*" In this the thief had an absolutely indisputable assurance that though he must die, yet he would live and find himself in paradise with his Lord.

I have thus shown you that our Lord passed within the pearly gate in company with one to whom He had pledged Himself. Why should not you and I pass through that pearl-gate in due time, clothed in His merit, washed in His blood, resting on His power? One of these days, angels will say of you and of me, "*Who is this that comes up from the wilderness, leaning upon her beloved?*" (Song of Solomon 8:5). The shining ones will be amazed to see some of us coming. If you have lived a life of sin until now, and yet shall repent and enter heaven, what an amazement there will be in every golden street to think that you have come there!

In the early Christian church, Marcus Caius Victorinus was converted; but he had reached so great an age, and had been so gross a sinner, that the pastor and church doubted him. He gave, however, clear proof of having undergone the divine change, and then there were great acclamations, and many shouts of "Victorinus has become a Christian!" Oh, that some of you big sinners might be saved! How gladly would we rejoice over you! Why not? Would it not glorify God? The salvation of this convicted highwayman has made our Lord illustrious for mercy even unto this day; would not your case do the same? Would not saints cry, "Hallelujah! Hallelujah!" if they heard that some of you had been turned from darkness to marvelous light? Why should it not be? Believe in Jesus, and it is so.

III. NOTE THE LORD'S SERMON TO US FROM ALL THIS

The devil wants to preach this morning a bit. Yes, Satan asks to come to the front and preach to you; but he cannot be allowed. Avaunt, you deceiver! Yet I should not wonder if he gets at certain of you when the sermon is over, and whispers, "You see? You can be saved at the very last. Put off repentance and faith; you may be forgiven on your deathbed." Sirs, you know who it is that would ruin you by this suggestion. Abhor his deceitful teaching. Do not be ungrateful because God is kind. Do not provoke the Lord because He is patient. Such conduct would be unworthy and ungrateful. Do not run an awful risk because one escaped the tremendous peril. The Lord will accept all who repent; but how do you know that you will repent? It is true that one thief was saved— but the other thief was lost. One is saved, and we may not despair; the other is lost, and we may not presume. Dear friends, I trust you are not made of such diabolical stuff as to fetch from the mercy of God an argument for continuing in sin. If you do, I can only say of you that your damnation will be just; you will have brought it upon yourselves.

Consider now the teaching of our Lord; see *the glory of Christ in salvation*. He is ready to save at the last moment. He was just passing away; His foot was on the doorstep of the Father's house. Up comes this poor sinner the last thing at night, at the eleventh hour, and the Savior smiles and declares that He will not enter except with this belated wanderer. At the very gate He declares that this seeking soul shall enter with Him. There was plenty of time for him to have come before. You know how apt we are to say, "You have waited to the last moment. I am just going off, and I cannot attend to you now." Our Lord has His dying pangs upon Him, and yet He attends to the perishing criminal and permits him to pass through the heavenly portal in His company. Jesus easily saves the sinners for whom He painfully died. Jesus loves to rescue sinners from going down into the pit. You will be very happy if you are saved, but you will not be one half so happy as He will be when He saves you. See how gentle He is!

> His hand no thunder bears,
> No terror clothes his brow;
> No bolts to drive our guilty souls
> To fiercer flames below.

He comes to us full of tenderness, with tears in His eyes, mercy in His hands, and love in His heart. Believe Him to be a great Savior of great sinners. I have heard of one who had received great mercy who went about saying, "He is a great forgiver"; and I would have you say the same. You shall find your transgressions put away, and your sins pardoned once for all, if you now trust Him.

The next doctrine Christ preaches from this wonderful story is *faith in its permitted attachment*. This man believed that Jesus was the Christ. The next thing he did was to appropriate that Christ. He said, *"Lord, remember me"* (Luke 23:42). Jesus might have said,

"What have I to do with you, and what have you to do with Me? What has a thief to do with the perfect One?" Many of you, good people, try to get as far away as you can from the erring and fallen. They might infect your innocence! Society claims that we should not be familiar with people who have offended against its laws. We must not be seen associating with them, for it might discredit us. Infamous bosh! Can anything discredit sinners such as we are, by nature and by practice? If we know ourselves before God, we are degraded enough in and of ourselves. Is there anybody, after all, in the world who is worse than we are when we see ourselves in the faithful glass of the Word? As soon as ever a man believes that Jesus is the Christ, let him hook himself onto Him. The moment you believe Jesus to be the Savior, seize upon Him as your Savior. If I remember rightly, Augustine called this man "*latro laudabilis et mirabilis,*" a thief to be praised and wondered at, who dared, as it were, to seize the Savior for his own. In this he is to be imitated. Take the Lord to be yours, and you have Him. Jesus is the common property of all sinners who make bold to take Him. Every sinner who has the will to do so may take the Lord home with him. He came into the world to save the sinful. (See Luke 19:10.) Take Him by force, as robbers take their prey; for the kingdom of heaven suffers the violence of daring faith. (See Matthew 11:12.) Get Him, and He will never get Himself away from you. If you trust Him, He must save you.

Next, notice the doctrine of *faith in its immediate power.*

The moment a sinner believes,
And trusts in his crucified God,
His pardon at once he receives,
Redemption in full through his blood.

"*Today shall you be with Me in paradise*" (Luke 23:43). He has no sooner believed than Christ gives him the seal of his believing in the full assurance that he shall be with Him forever in His glory. O dear hearts, if you believe this morning, you shall be saved this morning! God grant that you, by His rich grace, may be brought into salvation here, on the spot, and at once!

The next thing is *the nearness of eternal things*. Think of that a minute. Heaven and hell are not places far away. You may be in heaven before the clock ticks again, it is so near. Could we but rend that veil which parts us from the unseen! It is all there, and all near. *"Today,"* said the Lord—within three or four hours at the longest—*"shall you be with Me in paradise,"* so near is it. A statesman has given us the expression of being "within measurable distance." We are all within measurable distance of heaven or hell; if there be any difficulty in measuring the distance, it lies in its brevity rather than in its length.

> One gentle sigh the fetter breaks,
> We scarce can say, "He's gone,"
> Before the ransomed spirit takes
> Its mansion near the throne.

Oh, that we, instead of trifling about such things because they seem so far away, would solemnly realize them, since they are so very near! This very day, before the sun goes down, some hearer now sitting in this place may see, in his own spirit, the realities of heaven or hell. It has frequently happened in this large congregation that some one of our audience has died before the next Sabbath has come round. It may happen this week. Think of that, and let eternal things impress you all the more because they lie so near.

Furthermore, know that *if you have believed in Jesus, you are prepared for heaven*. It may be that you will have to live on earth twenty, or thirty, or forty years to glorify Christ; and, if so, be thankful for the privilege. But if you do not live another hour, your instantaneous death would not alter the fact that he that believeth in the Son of God is meet for heaven. Surely, if anything beyond faith is needed to make us fit to enter paradise, the thief would have been kept a little longer here; but, no, he is in the morning in the state of nature, at noon he enters the state of grace, and by sunset he is in the state of glory. The question never is whether a deathbed repentance is accepted if it be sincere; the question is, is it sincere? If it be so, if the man dies five minutes after his first act of faith, he is as safe as if he had served the Lord for fifty years. If your faith is true, if you die one moment after you have believed in Christ, you will be admitted into paradise, even if you shall have enjoyed no time in which to produce good works and other evidences of grace. He that reads the heart will read your faith written on its fleshy tablets, and He will accept you through Jesus Christ, even though no act of grace has been visible to the eye of man.

I conclude by again saying that *this is not an exceptional case.* I began with that, and I want to finish with it, because so many "demi-semi-gospellers" are so terribly afraid of preaching free grace too fully. I read somewhere, and I think it is true, that some ministers preach the gospel in the same way as donkeys eat thistles, namely, very, very cautiously. On the contrary, I will preach it boldly. I have not the slightest alarm about the matter. If any of you misuse free-grace teaching, I cannot help it. He that will be damned can as well ruin himself by perverting the gospel as by anything else. I cannot help what base hearts may invent; but mine it is to set forth the gospel in all its fullness of grace, and I will do it. If the thief was an exceptional case—and our Lord does not usually act in such a way—there would have been a hint given of so important a fact. A hedge would have been set about this exception to all rules. Would not the Savior have whispered quietly to the dying man, "You are the only one I am going to treat in this way"? Whenever I have to do an exceptional favor to a person, I have to say, "Do not mention this, or I shall have so many besieging me." If the Savior had meant this to be a solitary case, He would have faintly said to him, "Do not let anybody know; but you shall today be in the kingdom with Me." No, our Lord spoke openly, and those about Him heard what He said. Moreover, the inspired penman has recorded it. If it had been an exceptional case, it would not have been written in the Word of God. Men will not publish their actions in the newspapers if they feel that the record might lead others to expect from them what they cannot give. The Savior had this wonder of grace reported in the daily news of the gospel because He means to repeat the marvel every day. The bulk shall be equal to a sample, and therefore He sets the sample before you all. He is able to save to the uttermost, for He saved the dying thief. The case would not have been put there to encourage hopes which He cannot fulfill. Whatsoever things were written before time were written for our learning and not for our disappointing. I pray you, therefore, if any of you have not yet trusted in my Lord Jesus, come and trust in Him now. Trust Him wholly; trust Him only; trust Him at once. Then will you sing with me:

> The dying thief rejoiced to see
> That fountain in his day,
> And there have I, though vile as he,
> Washed all my sins away.

8

IT IS FINISHED!

"When Jesus therefore had received the vinegar, He said, It is finished: and He bowed His head, and gave up the ghost."
—John 19:30

My brethren, I would have you attentively observe the singular clearness, power, and quickness of the Savior's mind in the last agonies of death. When pains and groans attend the last hour, they frequently have the effect of discomposing the mind so that it is not possible for the dying man to collect his thoughts, or, having collected them, to utter them so that they can be understood by others. In no case could we expect a remarkable exercise of memory or a profound judgment upon deep subjects from an expiring man. But the Redeemer's last acts were full of wisdom and prudence, although His sufferings were beyond all measure excruciating.

Remark how clearly He perceived the significance of every type! How plainly He could read with dying eye those divine symbols which the eyes of angels could only desire to look into! He saw the secrets which have bewildered sages and astonished seers all fulfilled in His own body. Nor must we fail to observe the power and comprehensiveness by which He grasped the chain which binds the shadowy past with the sunlit present. We must not forget the brilliance of that intelligence which threaded all the ceremonies and sacrifices on one string of thought, beheld all the prophecies as one great revelation and all the promises as the heralds of one person, and then said of the whole, *"It is finished"* (John 19:30)—"finished in Me."

What quickness of mind was that which enabled Him to traverse all the centuries of prophecy, to penetrate the eternity of the covenant, and then to anticipate the eternal glories! And all this when He is mocked by multitudes of enemies and when His hands and feet are nailed to the cross. What force of mind must the Savior have possessed to soar above those "Alps of Agony" which touched the very clouds. In what a singular mental condition must He have been during the period of His crucifixion to be able to review the whole roll of inspiration! Now, this remark may not seem to be of any great value, but I think its value lies in certain inferences that may be drawn from it.

We have sometimes heard it said, "How could Christ, in so short a time, bear suffering which should be equivalent to the torments—the eternal torments of hell?" Our reply is that we are not capable of judging what the Son of God might do even in a moment, much less what He might do and what He might suffer in His life and in His death. It has been frequently affirmed by persons who have been rescued from drowning that the mind of a drowning man is singularly active. One who, after being some time in the water, was at last painfully restored has said that the whole of his history seemed to come before his mind while he was sinking, and that if anyone had asked him how long he had been in the water, he should have said twenty years, whereas he had only been there for a moment or two.

The wild romance of Mohammed's journey upon Alborak is not an unfitting illustration. He affirmed that when the angel came in vision to take him on his celebrated journey to Jerusalem, he went through all the seven heavens and saw all the wonders thereof. And yet he was gone so short a time that though the angel's wing had touched a basin of water when they started, they returned soon enough to prevent the water from being spilled. The long dream of this epileptic impostor may really have occupied but a second of time. The intellect of mortal man is such that if God wills it, when it is in certain states, it can think out centuries of thought at once. It can go through in one instant what we should have supposed would have taken years upon years of time for it to know or feel.

We think, therefore, that from the Savior's singular clearness and quickness of intellect upon the cross, it is very possible that He did in the space of two or three hours endure not only the agony which might have been contained in centuries but even an equivalent for that which might be comprehended in everlasting punishment. At any rate, it is not for us to say that it could not be so. When the Deity is arrayed in manhood, then manhood becomes omnipotent to suffer. And just as the feet of Christ were once almighty to tread the seas, so now was His whole body become almighty to dive into the great waters, to endure an immersion in "unknown agonies."

Do not, I pray, let us attempt to measure Christ's sufferings by the finite one of our own ignorant reason, but let us know and believe that what He endured there was accepted by God as an equivalent for all our pains. And, therefore, it could not have been a trifle but must have been all that Heart conceived it to be, when he says He bore...

All that incarnate God could bear,
With strength enough, but none to spare.

My discourse will, I have no doubt, more fully illustrate the remark with which I have commenced. Let us proceed to it at once.

First, let us hear the text and understand it. Then, let us hear it and wonder at it. And then, third, let us hear it and proclaim it.

I. LET US HEAR THE TEXT AND UNDERSTAND IT

The Son of God has been made Man. He has had a life of perfect virtue and of total self-denial. He has been all that life long despised and rejected of men, a Man of Sorrows and acquainted with grief. (See Isaiah 53:3.) His enemies have been legion. His friends have been few, and those few faithless. He is at last delivered over into the hands of them that hate Him. He is arrested while in the act of prayer. He is arraigned before both the spiritual and temporal courts. He is robed in mockery and then enrobed in shame. He is set upon His throne in scorn and then tied to the pillar in cruelty. He is declared innocent, and yet He is delivered up by the judge who ought to have preserved Him from His persecutors. (See Luke 23.)

He is dragged through the streets of that Jerusalem which had killed the prophets and would now crimson itself with the blood of the prophets' Master. He is brought to the cross. He is nailed fast to the cruel wood. The sun burns Him. His cruel wounds increase the fever. God forsakes Him. *"My God, My God, why have You forsaken Me?"* (Matthew 27:46) contains the concentrated anguish of the world. While He hangs there in mortal conflict with sin and Satan, His heart is broken, His limbs are dislocated. Heaven fails Him, for the sun is veiled in darkness. Earth forsakes Him, for *"the disciples forsook Him, and fled"* (Matthew 26:56). He looks everywhere, and there is none to help. He casts His eye around, and there is no man that can share His toil.

He treads the winepress alone. And of all the people there is none with Him. On, on He goes, steadily determined to drink the last dreg of that cup which must not pass from Him if His Father's will is done. At last He cries, *"It is finished"* (John 19:30), and He gives up the ghost. Hear it, Christians, hear this shout of triumph as it rings today with all the freshness and force which it had all those years ago! Hear it from the Sacred Word and from the Savior's lips, and may the Spirit of God open your ears, that you may hear as the learned and understand what you hear!

1. WHAT MEANT THE SAVIOR BY "IT IS FINISHED"?

He meant, first of all, that all the types, promises, and prophecies were now fully accomplished in Him. Those who are acquainted with the original will find that the words *"It is finished"* occur twice within three verses. In John 19:28, we have the word in the Greek. It is translated in our version as *"accomplished,"* but there it stands: *"After this, Jesus knowing that all things were now accomplished, that the Scripture might be fulfilled, says, 'I thirst'"* (John 19:28). And then He afterward said, *"It is finished."* This leads us to see His meaning very clearly—that all the Scripture was now fulfilled; that when He said, *"It is finished,"* the whole Book, from the first to the last, in both the law and the prophets, was finished in Him.

There is not a single jewel of promise, from that first emerald which fell on the threshold of Eden to that last sapphire-stone of Malachi, which was not set in the breastplate of the true High Priest. No, there is not a type, from the red heifer downward to the turtledove, from the hyssop upward to Solomon's temple itself, which was not fulfilled in Him. And not a prophecy, whether spoken on Chebar's bank or on the shores of Jordan, not a dream of wise men—whether they had received it in Babylon, or in Samaria, or in Judea—which was not now fully worked out in Christ Jesus. And, brethren, what a wonderful thing it is, that a mass of promises and prophecies and types apparently so heterogeneous should all be accomplished in one person!

Take away Christ for one moment, and I will give the Old Testament to any wise man living and say to him, "Take this. This is a problem. Go home and construct in your imagination an ideal character who shall exactly fit all that which is herein foreshadowed. Remember, He must be a prophet like unto Moses and yet a champion like Joshua. He must be an Aaron and a Melchisedec. He must be both David and Solomon, Noah, and Jonah, Judah, and Joseph. No, He must not only be the lamb that was slain and the scapegoat that was not slain, the turtledove that was dipped in blood and the priest who slew the bird, but He must be the altar, the tabernacle, the mercy seat, and the showbread."

No, to puzzle this wise man further, we remind him of prophecies so apparently contradictory that one would think they never could meet in one man. "*All kings shall fall down before him: all nations shall serve him*" (Psalm 72:11), and yet He is "*despised and rejected of men*" (Isaiah 53:3). He must begin by showing a man born of a virgin mother: "*A virgin shall conceive, and bear a son*" (Isaiah 7:14). He must be a man without spot or blemish (see 1 Peter 1:19) but yet one be one upon whom the Lord does cause to meet the iniquities of us all (see Isaiah 53:6.) He must be a glorious one, a Son of David, but yet a root out of a dry ground. (See Isaiah 53:2.) Now I say it boldly: if all the greatest intellects of all the ages could set themselves to work out this problem, to invent another key to the types and prophecies, they could not do it.

I see you, you wise men—you are poring over these hieroglyphs. One suggests one key, and it opens two or three of the figures. But you cannot proceed, for the next one puts you at a nonplus. Another learned man suggests another clue, but that fails most where it is most needed—and another and another, and thus these wondrous hieroglyphs traced of old by Moses in the wilderness must be left unexplained, till one comes forward and proclaims, "The cross of Christ and the Son of God incarnate"— then the whole is clear, so that he that runs may read, and a child may understand.

Blessed Savior! In You we see everything fulfilled which God spoke of in old by the prophets. In You we discover everything carried out in substance which God had set before us in the dim mist of sacrificial smoke. Glory be unto Your name! *"It is finished"*— everything is summed up in You.

2. ALL THE TYPICAL SACRIFICES OF THE OLD JEWISH LAW WERE NOW ABOLISHED AND EXPLAINED

The words *"It is finished"* have richer meaning. Not only were all types and prophecies and promises thus finished in Christ, but all the typical sacrifices of the old Jewish law were now abolished as well as explained.

They were finished—finished in Him. Will you imagine for a minute the saints in heaven looking down upon what was done on earth—Abel and his friends, who had long ago before the flood been sitting in the glories above? They watch while God lights star after star in heaven. Promise after promise flashes light upon the thick darkness of earth. They see Abraham come, and they look down and wonder while they see God revealing Christ to Abraham in the person of Isaac. They gaze just as the angels do, desiring to look into the mystery. (See 1 Peter 1:12.) From the times of Noah, Abraham, Isaac, and Jacob, they see altars smoking, recognitions of the fact that man is guilty, and the spirits before the throne say, "Lord, when will sacrifices finish? When will blood no more be shed?"

The offering of bloody sacrifices soon increases. It is now carried on by men ordained for the purpose. Aaron and the high priests and the Levites every morning and every evening offer a lamb, while great sacrifices are offered on special occasions. Bullocks groan, rams bleed, the necks of doves are wrung; and all the while, the saints are crying, "O Lord, how long? When shall the sacrifice cease?" Year after year the high priest goes within the veil and sprinkles the mercy seat with blood. The next year sees him do the like, and the next, and again and again and again.

David offers hecatombs; Solomon slaughters tens of thousands. Hezekiah offers rivers of oil; Josiah gives thousands of the fat of fed beasts; and the spirits of the just say, "Will it never be complete? Will the sacrifice never be finished? Must there always be a remembrance of sin? Will not the last High Priest soon come? Will not the order and line of Aaron soon lay aside its labor, because the whole is finished?" Not yet, not yet, you spirits of the just—for after the captivity the slaughter of victims still remains. But lo, He comes! Gaze more intently than before—He comes who is to close the line of priests! Lo, there He stands, clothed—not now with linen ephod, not with ringing bells, nor with sparkling jewels on His breastplate, but arrayed in human flesh He stands!

His cross, His altar; His body and His soul, the victim; Himself, the Priest; and—lo! Before His God He offers up His own soul within the veil of thick darkness which has covered Him from the sight of men. Presenting His own blood, He enters within the veil, sprinkles it there, and, coming forth from the midst of the darkness, He looks down on the astonished earth and upward to expectant heaven and cries, "It is finished! It is finished!" That for which you looked so long is fully achieved and perfected forever!

3. PERFECT OBEDIENCE WAS FINISHED

The Savior meant, we doubt not, that in this moment His perfect obedience was finished. It was necessary, in order that man might be saved, that the law of God should be kept—for no man can see God's face except that he be perfect in righteousness. Christ undertook to keep God's law for His people, to obey its every mandate and preserve its every statute intact. Throughout the first years of His life, He privately obeyed, honoring His father and His mother. During the next three years He publicly obeyed God, spending and being spent in His service, till if you would know what a man would be whose life was wholly conformed to the law of God, you may see him in Christ.

My dear Redeemer and my Lord,
I read my duty in Your Word,

But in Your life the law appears
Drawn out in living characters.

It needed nothing to complete the perfect virtue of life but the entire obedience of death. He who would serve God must be willing not only to give all his soul and his strength while he lives, but he must stand prepared to resign life when it shall be for God's glory. Our perfect Substitute put the last stroke upon His work by dying, and therefore He claims to be absolved from further debt, for "It is finished." Yes, glorious Lamb of God, it is finished! You have been tempted in all points like as we are, yet have You sinned in none! It was finished, for the last arrow out of Satan's quiver had been shot at You. The last blasphemous insinuation, the last wicked temptation, had spent its fury on You.

The prince of this world had surveyed You from head to foot, within and without, but he had found nothing in You. Now Your trial is over—You have finished the work which Your Father gave You to do and so finished it that hell itself cannot accuse You of a flaw. And now, looking upon Your entire obedience, You say, "It is finished," and we Your people believe most joyously that it is even so. Brothers and sisters, this is more than you or I could have said if Adam had never fallen. If we had been in the garden of Eden today, we could never have boasted a finished righteousness, since a creature can never finish its obedience.

As long as a creature lives, it is bound to obey, and as long as a free agent exists on earth, it would be in danger of violating the vow of its obedience. If Adam had been in paradise from the first day until now, he might fall tomorrow. Left to himself, there would be no reason why that king of nature should not yet be uncrowned. But Christ the Creator, who finished creation, has perfected redemption. God can ask no more. The law has received all it claims; the largest extent of justice cannot demand another hour's obedience. It is done, it is complete. The last throw of the shuttle is over, and the robe is woven from the top throughout. Let us rejoice, then, in this: that the Master meant by His dying cry that His perfect righteousness wherewith He covers us was finished.

4. GOD'S JUSTICE WAS SATISFIED

Next, the Savior meant that the satisfaction which He rendered to the justice of God was finished. The debt was now, to the last farthing, all discharged. The atonement and propitiation were made once and for all and forever by the one offering made in Jesus's body on the tree. There was the cup, hell was in it, the Savior drank it—not a sip and then a pause; not a draught and then a ceasing. He drained it till there was not a dreg left for any of His people. The great ten-thronged whip of the law was worn out upon His back. There is no lash left with which to smite one for whom Jesus died. The great cannonade of God's justice has exhausted all its ammunition—there is nothing left to be hurled against a child of God.

Sheathed is your sword, O justice! Silenced is your thunder, O law! There remains nothing now of all the griefs and pains and agonies which chosen sinners ought to have suffered for their sins, for Christ has endured all for His own beloved, and *"It is finished."* Brethren, it is more than the damned in hell can ever say. If you and I had been constrained to make satisfaction to God's justice by being sent to hell, we never could have said, "It is finished." Christ has paid the debt which all the torments of eternity could not have paid. Lost souls, you suffer today as you have suffered for ages past, but God's justice is not satisfied; His law is not fully magnified.

And when time shall fail and eternity shall have been flying on still forever, the uttermost never having been paid, the chastisement for sin must fall upon unpardoned sinners. But Christ has done what all the flames of the pit could not do in all eternity. He has magnified the law and made it honorable, and now from the cross He cries, "It is finished."

5. SATAN IS CONQUERED

Once again, when He said, "It is finished," Jesus had totally destroyed the power of Satan, of sin, and of death. The Champion had entered the lists to do battle for our soul's redemption against all our foes. He met sin. Horrible, terrible, all-but omnipotent sin nailed Him to the cross. But in that deed, Christ nailed sin also to the tree. There they both did hang together—sin and Sin's Destroyer. Sin destroyed Christ, and by that destruction, Christ destroyed sin. Next came the second enemy, Satan. He assaulted Christ with all his hosts. Calling up his myrmidons from every corner and quarter of the universe, he said, "Awake, arise, or be forever fallen! Here is our great Enemy who has sworn to bruise my head. Now let us bruise His heel!" (See Genesis 3:15.)

They shot their hellish darts into His heart. They poured their boiling cauldrons on His brain; they emptied their venom into His veins. They spat their insinuations into His face. They hissed their devilish fears into His ear. He stood alone, the Lion of the tribe of Judah, hounded by all the dogs of hell. Our Champion quailed not but used His holy weapons, striking right and left with all the power of God-supported manhood. On came the hosts; volley after volley was discharged against Him. No mimic thunders were these, but such as might shake the very gates of hell. The Conqueror steadily advanced, overturning their ranks, dashing in pieces His enemies, breaking the bow, cutting the spear in sunder, and burning the chariots in the fire, while He cried, "In the name of God will I destroy you!" (See Psalm 118:10.)

At last, foot to foot, He met the champion of hell, and now our David fought with Goliath. Not long was the struggle. Thick was the darkness which gathered round them both. But He who is the Son of God, as well as the Son of Mary, knew how to smite the fiend, and He did smite him with divine fury, till, having despoiled him of his armor, having quenched his fiery darts and broken his head, He cried, *"It is finished"* and sent the fiend, bleeding and howling, down to bed. We can imagine him pursued by the eternal Savior, who exclaims:

Traitor!
My bolt shall find and pierce you through,
Though under hell's profoundest wave
You div'st, to seek a sheltering grave.

His thunderbolt overtook the fiend, and, grasping him with both His hands, the Savior drew around him the great chain. The angels brought the royal chariot from on high, to whose wheels the captive fiend was bound. Lash the coursers up the everlasting hills! Spirits made perfect, come forth to meet Him. Sing to the Conqueror who drags death and hell behind Him and leads captivity captive! "Lift up your heads, O you gates, and be you lifted up, you everlasting doors, that the King of glory may come in." (See Psalm 24:9.) But stay—before He enters, let Him be rid of this His burden. Lo, He takes the fiend and hurls him down through illimitable night, broken, bruised, with his power destroyed, bereft of his crown, to lie forever howling in the pit of hell.

Thus, when the Savior cried, *"It is finished,"* He had defeated sin and Satan—nor less had He vanquished death. Death had come against Him, as Christmas Evans puts it, with his fiery dart which he struck right through the Savior, till the point fixed in the cross. And when he tried to pull it out again, he left the sting behind. What could he do more? He was disarmed. Then Christ set some of his prisoners free, for many of the saints arose and were seen of many. Then He said to him, "Death, I take from you your keys—you must live for a little while to be the warden of those beds in which My saints shall sleep, but give Me your keys."

And lo, the Savior stands today with the keys of death hanging at His girdle, and He waits until the hour shall come of which no man knows, when the trumpet of the archangel shall ring like the silver trumpets of Jubilee, and then He shall say, "Let My captives go free." (See Isaiah 45:13.) Then shall the tombs be opened in virtue of Christ's death, and the very bodies of the saints shall live again in an eternity of glory.

"It is finished!"
Hear the dying Savior cry.

II. *"IT IS FINISHED"*: LET US HEAR AND WONDER

Let us perceive what mighty things were effected and secured by these words, *"It is finished."* Thus He ratified the covenant. That covenant was signed and sealed before, and in all things it was ordered well, but when Christ said, *"It is finished,"* then the covenant was made doubly sure, when the blood of Christ's heart bespattered the divine roll. Then it could never be reversed, nor could one of its ordinances be broken, nor one of its stipulations fail. You know of the everlasting covenant—God covenants on His part that He would give Christ to see of the travail of His soul, that all who were given to Him should have new hearts and right spirits. They should be washed from sin and should enter into life through Him.

Christ's side of the covenant was this: "Father, I will do Your will. I will pay the ransom to the last jot and tittle. (See Matthew 5:18.) I will give You perfect obedience and complete satisfaction." Now, if this second part of the covenant had never been fulfilled, the first part would have been invalid—but when Jesus said, *"It is finished,"* then there was nothing left to be performed on His part; now the covenant is all on one side. It is God's "I will" and "They shall." *"A new heart also will I give you, and a new Spirit will*

I put within you" (Ezekiel 36:26). "*Then will I sprinkle clean water upon you, and you shall be clean*" (Ezekiel 36:25). "From all your iniquities will I cleanse you." (See Ezekiel 36:33.) "I will lead you by a way that you know not." (See Isaiah 42:16.) "I will surely bring them in."

The covenant that day was ratified. When Christ said, "*It is finished,*" His Father was honored, and divine justice was fully displayed. The Father always did love His people. Do not think that Christ died to make God the Father loving. He always had loved them from before the foundation of the world, but "*It is finished*" took away the barriers which were in the Father's way. He would, as a God of love—and now He could, as a God of justice—bless poor sinners. From that day the Father is well-pleased to receive sinners to His bosom. When Christ said, "*It is finished,*" He Himself was glorified. Then on His head descended the all-glorious crown. Then did the Father give to Him honors which He had not before. He had honor as God, but as Man He was despised and rejected—now as God and Man, Christ was made to sit down forever on His Father's throne, crowned with honor and majesty. Then, too, by "*It is finished,*" the Spirit was procured for us:

> 'Tis by the merit of His death
> Who hung upon the tree,
> The Spirit is sent down to breathe
> On such dry bones as we.

Then the Spirit which Christ had before time promised perceived a new and living way by which He could come to dwell in the hearts of men, and men might come up to dwell with Him above. That day, too, when Christ said, "*It is finished,*" the words had effect on heaven. Then the walls of chrysolite stood fast. Then the jasper-light of the pearly-gated city shone like the light of seven days. Before, the saints had been saved, as it were, on credit. They had entered heaven, God having faith in His Son Jesus. Had not Christ finished His work, surely, they must have left their shining spheres and suffered in their own persons for their own sins.

I might represent heaven, if my imagination might be allowed a moment, as being ready to totter if Christ had not finished His work—its stones would have been unloosed, massive and stupendous though its bastions are. Yet they would have fallen as earthly cities reel under the throes of earthquake. But Christ said, "It is finished," and oath, and covenant, and blood set fast the dwelling place of the redeemed, made their mansions safely and eternally their own, and bade their feet stand immovably upon the rock. No, even more: that word, "It is finished!" took effect in the gloomy caverns and depths of hell. Then Satan bit his iron bands in a rage, howling, "I am defeated by the very Man whom I thought to overcome! My hopes are blasted. Never shall an elect one come into my prison, never a blood-bought one be found in my abode."

Lost souls mourned that day, for they said, "It is finished! And if Christ Himself, the Substitute, could not be permitted to go free till He had finished all His punishment, then we shall never be free." It was their double death-knell, for they said, "Alas for us! Justice, which would not suffer the Savior to escape, will never suffer us to be at liberty. It is finished with Him, and therefore it shall never be finished for us." That day, too, the earth had a gleam of sunlight cast over her which she had never known before. Then her hilltops began to glisten with the rising of the sun.

And though her valleys still are clothed with darkness, and men wander here and there and grope in the noonday as in the night (see Job 5:14), yet that sun is rising, climbing still its heavenly steeps, never to set, and soon shall its rays penetrate through the thick mists and clouds, and every eye shall see Him, and every heart be made glad with His light. The words "It is finished" consolidated heaven, shook hell, comforted earth, delighted the Father, glorified the Son, brought down the Spirit, and confirmed the everlasting covenant to all the chosen seed.

III. *"IT IS FINISHED"*: LET US PUBLISH IT

Children of God, you who by faith received Christ as your All in All, tell it every day of your lives, *"It is finished."* Go and tell it to those who are torturing themselves, thinking through obedience and mortification to offer satisfaction. Yonder Hindu is about to throw himself down upon the spikes. Stay, poor man! Why would you bleed, for *"it is finished"*? Yonder Fakir is holding his hand erect till the nails grow through the flesh, torturing himself with fasting and with self-denials. Cease, cease, poor wretch, from all these pains, for *"it is finished"*!

In all parts of the earth there are those who think that the misery of the body and the soul may be an atonement for sin. Rush to them, stay them in their madness, and say to them, "Why do you this? 'It is finished.'" All the pains that God asks, Christ has suffered. All the satisfaction by way of agony in the flesh that the law demands, Christ has already endured. "It is finished!" And when you have done this, go next to the benighted votaries of Rome when you see the priests with their backs to the people, offering every day the pretended sacrifice of the mass and lifting up the host on high—a sacrifice, they say—"an unbloody sacrifice for the quick and the dead." Cry to them, "Cease, false priest, cease! For 'it is finished'! Cease, false worshipper, cease to bow, for 'it is finished'!"

God neither asks nor accepts any other sacrifice than that which Christ offered once for all upon the cross. Go next to the those among your own countrymen who call themselves Protestants but who are Papists after all—who think by their gifts and their gold, by their prayers and their vows, by their churchgoings and their chapel-goings, by their baptisms and their confirmations, to make themselves fit for God. And say to them, "Stop. *It is finished.'* God needs not this of you. He has received enough. Why will you pin your rags to the fine linen of Christ's righteousness? Why will you add your counterfeit farthing to the costly ransom which Christ has paid into the treasure-house of God? Cease from your pains, your doings, your performances. *'It is finished'*! Christ has done it all."

This one text is enough to blow the Vatican to the four winds. Lay but this beneath Popery and, like a train of gunpowder beneath a rock, it shall blast it into the air. This is a thunderclap against all human righteousness. Only let this come like a two-edged sword, and your good works and your fine performances are soon cast away. *"It is finished."* Why improve on what is finished? Why add to that which is complete? The Bible is finished—he that adds to it never had his name in the Book of Life and will never see the Holy City. (See Revelation 22:18–19.) Christ's atonement is finished, and he that adds to that must expect the selfsame doom.

And when you shall have told it thus to the ears of men of every nation and of every tribe, tell it to all poor despairing souls. You find them on their knees, crying, "O God, what can I do to make recompense for my offenses?" Tell them, *"It is finished,"* the recompense is made already. "O God!" they say. "How can I ever get a righteousness in which You can accept such a worm as I am?" Tell them, *"It is finished"*; their righteousness is worked out already. They have no need to trouble themselves about adding to it. *"It is finished."*

Go to the poor despairing wretch who has given himself up, not for death merely, but for damnation—he who says, "I cannot escape from sin, and I cannot be saved from its punishment." Say to him, "Sinner, the way of salvation is finished once and for all." And if you meet some professed Christians in doubts and fears, tell them, *"It is finished."* Why, we have hundreds and thousands that are converted who do not know that *"it is finished."* They never know that they are safe. They do not know that *"it is finished."*

They think they have faith today, but perhaps they may become unbelieving tomorrow. They do not know that *"it is finished."*

They hope God will accept them if they do some things, forgetting that the way of acceptance is finished. God as much accepts a sinner who only believed in Christ five minutes ago as He will a saint who has known and loved Him eighty years, for He does not accept men because of anything they do or feel but simply and only for what Christ did, and that is finished. Oh, poor hearts! Some of you do love the Savior in a measure, but blindly. You are thinking that you must be this and attain to that, and then you may be assured that you are saved.

Oh, you may be assured of it today—if you believe in Christ, you are saved. "But I feel imperfections." Yes, but what of that? God does not regard your imperfections—He covers them with Christ's righteousness. He sees them to remove them, but not to lay them to your charge. "Yes, but I cannot be what I would be." But what if you cannot? God does not look at you as what you are in yourself but as what you are in Christ.

Come with me, poor soul, and you and I will stand together this morning while the tempest gathers, for we are not afraid. How sharp that lightning flash! But yet we tremble not. How terrible that peal of thunder! And yet we are not alarmed. And why? Is there anything in us why we should escape? No, but we are standing beneath the cross, that precious cross, which, like some noble lightning rod in the storm, takes to itself all the death from the lightning and all the fury from the storm. We are safe. Loud may you roar, O thundering law, and terribly may you flash, O avenging justice; we can look up with calm delight to all the tumult of the elements, for we are safe beneath the cross.

Come with me again. There is a royal banquet spread. The King Himself sits at the table, and angels are the servitors. Let us enter. And we do enter, and we sit down, and eat, and drink; but how dare we do this? Our righteousnesses are as filthy rags (see

Isaiah 64:6)—how could we venture to come here? Oh, because the filthy rags are not ours any longer. We have renounced our own righteousness, and therefore we have renounced the filthy rags. And now, today, we wear the royal garments of the Savior and are from head to foot arrayed in white, without spot or wrinkle or any such thing. We stand in the clear sunlight—black, but comely; loathsome in ourselves, but glorious in Him! Condemned in Adam but accepted in the beloved. (See Ephesians 1:6.) We are neither afraid nor ashamed to be with the angels of God, to talk with the glorified, no, nor even alarmed to speak with God Himself and call Him our Friend.

And now, last of all, I publish this to sinners. I know not where you are this morning, but may God find you out. You who have been a drunkard, swearer, thief; you who have been a blackguard of the blackest kind; you who have dived into the very kennel and rolled yourself in the mire—if today you feel that sin is hateful to you, believe in Him who has said, "It is finished." Let me link your hand in mine, let us come together, both of us, and say, "Here are two poor naked souls, good Lord; we cannot clothe ourselves." And He will give us a robe, for "it is finished." "But, Lord, is it long enough for such sinners and broad enough for such offenders?" "Yes," says He, "it is finished."

"But we need washing, Lord! Is there anything that can take away black spots so hideous as ours?" "Yes," says He, "here is the bath of blood." "But must we not add our tears to it?" "No," says He, "no, it is finished. That is enough." "And now, Lord, You have washed us, and You have clothed us, but we desire to be completely clean within, so that we may never sin anymore. Lord, is there a way by which this can be done?" "Yes," says He, "there is the bath of water which flows from the wounded side of Christ." "And, Lord, is there enough there to wash away my guiltiness as well as my guilt?" "Yes," says He, "it is finished. Jesus Christ is made unto you sanctification as well as redemption." (See 1 Corinthians 1:30.)

Child of God, will you have Christ's finished righteousness this morning, and will you rejoice in it more than you have ever done before? And oh, poor sinner, will you have Christ or nothing? "Ah," says one, "I am willing enough, but I am not worthy." He does not want any worthiness. All He asks is willingness, for you know how He puts it: "Whoever will, let him come." (See Revelation 22:17.) If He has given you willingness, you may believe in Christ's finished work this morning. "Ah," you say, "but you cannot mean me." But I do, for it says, *"Ho, everyone that thirsts"* (Isaiah 55:1).

Do you thirst for Christ? Do you wish to be saved by Him? *"Everyone that thirsts"*—not only that young woman yonder, not simply that gray-headed old rebel yonder who has long despised the Savior, but this mass below, and you in these double tiers of gallery: *"Every one that thirsts, come you to the waters, and he that has no money; come…"* (Isaiah 55:1). O that I could "compel" you to come! Great God, won't You make the sinner willing to be saved? He wills to be damned—and will not come unless You change his will! Eternal Spirit, source of light, and life, and grace, come down and bring the strangers home!

"It is finished." Sinner, there is nothing for God to do. *"It is finished."* There is nothing for you to do. *"It is finished."* "Christ need not bleed." It is finished. "You need not weep." *"It is finished."* God the Holy Spirit need not tarry because of your unworthiness, nor need you tarry because of your helplessness. *"It is finished."* Every stumbling block is rolled out of the road, every gate is opened, the bars of brass are broken, the gates of iron are burst asunder.

"It is finished"! Come and welcome, come, and welcome! The table is laid, the fatlings are killed, the oxen are ready. Lo, here stands the messenger! Come from the highways and from the hedges! Come from the dens and from the kens of London. Come, you vilest of the vile. You who hate yourselves today, come! Jesus bids you! Oh, will you tarry? Oh, Spirit of God, won't You repeat the invitation and make it an effectual call to many a heart, for Jesus's sake! Amen.

9

THE CROSS, OUR GLORY

"But God forbid that I should glory, save in the cross of our
Lord Jesus Christ, by whom the world is crucified to me,
and I to the world."
—Galatians 6:14

Almost all men have something in which to glory. Every bird has its own note of song. It is a poor heart that never rejoices. It is a dull packhorse that is altogether without bells. Men usually rejoice in something or other, and many men so rejoice in that which they choose that they become boastful and full of vainglory. It is very sad that men should be ruined by their glory, and yet, many are. Many glory in their shame, and more glory in that which is mere emptiness. Some glory in their physical strength, in which an ox excels them; or in their gold, which is but thick clay; or in their gifts, which are but talents with which they are entrusted. The pounds entrusted to their stewardship are thought, by men, to belong to themselves, and therefore they rob God of the glory of them. O my hearers, hear the voice of wisdom, which cries, *"He that glories, let him glory in the Lord"* (1 Corinthians 1:31). To live for personal glory is to be dead while we live! Be not so foolish as to perish for a bubble! Many a man has thrown his soul away for a little honor or for the transient satisfaction of success in trifles. O men, your tendency is to glory in something—your wisdom will be to find a glory worthy of an immortal mind!

The apostle Paul had a rich choice of things in which he could have gloried. If it had been his mind to have remained among his own people, he might have been one of their most honored rabbis. He says, "*If any other man thinks that he has whereof he might trust in the flesh, I more: circumcised the eighth day, of the stock of Israel, of the tribe of Benjamin, a Hebrew of the Hebrews; as touching the law, a Pharisee; concerning zeal, persecuting the church; touching the righteousness which is in the law, blameless*" (Philippians 3:4–6). He says that he profited in the Jews' religion above many of his equals in his own nation and he stood high in the esteem of his fellow professors. But when he was converted to the faith of the Lord Jesus, he said, "*What things were gain to me, those I counted loss for Christ. Yea doubtless, and I count all things but loss for the excellency of the knowledge of Christ Jesus my* LORD" (Philippians 3:7–8). As soon as he was converted, he forsook all boasting in his former religion and zeal, and cried, "God forbid that I should glory in my birth, my education, my proficiency in Scripture, or my regard to orthodox ritual." "*God forbid that I should glory, save in the cross of our* LORD *Jesus Christ*" (Galatians 6:14).

Paul might also, if he had chosen, have gloried in his sufferings for the cross of Christ, for he had been a living martyr, a perpetual self-sacrifice to the cause of the crucified. He says:

> *Are they ministers of Christ? (I speak as a fool) I am more; in labors more abundant, in stripes above measure, in prisons more frequent, in deaths often. Of the Jews five times received I forty stripes save one. Thrice was I beaten with rods, once was I stoned, thrice I suffered shipwreck, a night and a day I have been in the deep; in journeyings often, in perils of waters, in perils of robbers, in perils by my own countrymen, in perils*

by the heathen, in perils in the city, in perils in the wilderness,
in perils in the sea, in perils among false brethren; in weari-
ness and painfulness, in watchings often, in hunger and thirst,
in fastings often, in cold and nakedness.

(2 Corinthians 11:23–27)

He was once driven to give a summary of these sufferings to establish his apostleship, but before he did so, he wrote, *"Would to God you could bear with me a little in my folly"* (2 Corinthians 11:1). In his heart he was saying, all the while, *"God forbid that I should glory, save in the cross of our LORD Jesus Christ"* (Galatians 6:14).

The great apostle had yet another reason for glorying, if he had chosen to do so, for he could speak of visions and revelations of the Lord. He says, *"I knew a man in Christ above fourteen years ago. . . such a one caught up to the third heaven. And I knew such a man. . . How that he was caught up into paradise, and heard unspeakable words, which it is not lawful for a man to utter"* (2 Corinthians 12:2–4). He was in danger of being exalted above measure by reason of the abundance of these revelations and, therefore, he was humbled by a painful thorn in the flesh. Paul, when hard driven by the necessity to maintain his position in the Corinthian Church, was forced to mention these things—but he liked not such glorying—he was most at ease when he said, *"God forbid that I should glory, save in the cross of our LORD Jesus Christ"* (Galatians 6:14).

Brothers and sisters, notice that Paul does not here say that he gloried in Christ, though he did so with all his heart—he declares that he gloried most in *"the cross of our LORD Jesus Christ,"* which, in the eyes of men, was the very lowest and most inglorious part of the history of the Lord Jesus! He could have gloried in the incarnation—angels sang of it; wise men came from the Far East to behold it. Did not the newborn King awake the song from heaven of *"Glory to God in the highest"* (Luke 2:14)? He might have gloried in the life of Christ—was there ever such another so benevolent and blameless? He might have gloried in the resurrection of Christ—it is the world's great hope concerning those that are asleep. He might have gloried in our Lord's ascension, for He *"led captivity captive"* (Ephesians 4:8), and all His followers glory in His victory. He might have gloried in His second advent, and I doubt not that he did, for the Lord shall soon descend from heaven with a shout, with the voice of the archangel and the trumpet of God (see 1 Thessalonians 4:16), to be admired in all them that believe.

Yet the apostle selected beyond all these that center of the Christian system, that point which is most assailed by its foes, that focus of the world's derision—the cross—and, putting all else somewhat into the shade, he exclaims, *"God forbid that I should glory, save in the cross of our* Lord *Jesus Christ"* (Galatians 6:14). Learn, then, that the highest glory of our holy religion is the cross! The history of grace begins earlier and goes on later, but in its middle point stands the cross. Of two eternities this is the hinge—of past decrees and future glories this is the pivot. Let us come to the cross this morning and think of it till each one of us, in the power of the Spirit of God, shall say, *"God forbid that I should glory, save in the cross of our* Lord *Jesus Christ."*

I. WHAT DID PAUL MEAN BY "THE CROSS"?

Did he not include, under this term, first, the fact of the cross; second, the doctrine of the cross; and, third, the cross of the doctrine?

1. THE FACT OF THE CROSS

Our Lord Jesus Christ did really die upon a gallows, the death of a felon. He was literally put to death upon a tree, accursed in the esteem of men. I beg you to notice how the apostle Paul puts it—*"the cross of our* Lord *Jesus Christ."* In his epistles, he sometimes says, "Christ"; at another times, "Jesus"; frequently, "Lord";

and oftentimes, "our Lord": but here he says, "*Our* LORD *Jesus Christ*." There is a sort of pomp of words in this full description, as if in contrast to the shame of the cross. The terms are intended, in some small measure, to express the dignity of Him who was put to so ignominious a death. He is Christ the Anointed and Jesus the Savior. He is the Lord, the Lord of All, and He is "*our* LORD *Jesus Christ*." He is not a Lord without subjects, for He is "*our* LORD." Nor is He a Savior without saved ones, for He is "*our* LORD *Jesus*." Nor has He the anointing for Himself only, for all of us have a share in Him as "*our…Christ*." In all, He is ours, and was so upon the cross.

When they bury a great nobleman, a herald stands at the head of the grave and proclaims his titles. "Here lies the body of William, Duke of this, and Earl of that, and Count of the other, knight of this order and commander of the other." Even thus, in deep solemnity, with brevity and fullness, Paul proclaims, beneath the bitter tree, the names and titles of the Savior of men and styles Him as "*our* LORD *Jesus Christ*." There are enough words here to give a foursquare description of the honor, dignity, and majesty of Him who has both Godhead and Manhood, who "*bore our sins in His own body on the tree*" (1 Peter 2:24). Be it forever had in reverent remembrance that He who died upon the cross between two thieves counted it not robbery to be equal with God! (See Philippians 2:5–8.) By nature He is such that the Nicene Creed well describes Him as "Begotten of His Father before all worlds, God of God, Light of Light, very God of very God." Yet He "*made Himself of no reputation, and took upon Him the form of a servant… and became obedient to death, even the death of the cross*" (Philippians 2:7, 8). I declare this fact to you in words, but I think them poor, dumb things. I wish I could speak this matchless truth in fire-flakes! The announcement that the Son of God died upon the cross to save men deserves the accompaniment of angelic trumpets and of the harps of the redeemed!

2. THE DOCTRINE OF THE CROSS

What is that doctrine of the cross, of which it is written that it is to them that perish foolishness, but to us which are saved it is the power of God and the wisdom of God? (See 1 Corinthians 1:18, 24). In one word, it is the doctrine of the atonement—the doctrine that the Lord Jesus Christ was made sin for us, that Christ was once offered to bear the sins of many, and that God has set Him forth to be the propitiation for our sins. Paul says, *"When we were yet without strength, in due time Christ died for the ungodly"* (Romans 5:6). And again, *"Now once in the end of the world has He appeared to put away sin by the sacrifice of Himself"* (Hebrews 9:26). The doctrine of the cross is that of sacrifice for sin—Jesus is *"the Lamb of God, which takes away the sin of the world"* (John 1:29). *"God so loved the world, that He gave His only begotten Son, that whosoever believes in Him should not perish, but have everlasting life"* (John 3:16). The doctrine is that of a full atonement made and the utmost ransom paid. *"Christ has redeemed us from the curse of the law, being made a curse for us: for it is written, Cursed is every one that hangs on a tree"* (Galatians 3:13). In Christ upon the cross, we see the just dying for the unjust, that He might bring us to God (see 1 Peter 3:18)—the Innocent bearing the crimes of the guilty, that they might be forgiven and accepted. That is the doctrine of the cross, of which Paul was never ashamed. (See Romans 1:16.)

This also is a necessary part of the doctrine—that whoever believes in Him is justified from all sin. (See Acts 13:39.) Whoever trusts in the Lord Jesus Christ is, in that moment, forgiven, justified, and accepted in the beloved. *"As Moses lifted up the serpent in the wilderness, even so must the Son of man be lifted up: that whosoever believes in Him should not perish, but have eternal life"* (John 3:14–15). Paul's doctrine was this: *"It is not of him that wills, nor of him that runs, but of God that shows mercy"* (Romans 9:16). And it was his constant teaching that salvation is not of works, nor of ceremonies, but simply and only by believing in Jesus! We are to

accept, by an act of trust, that righteousness which is already finished and completed by the death of our blessed Lord upon the
cross. He who does not preach atonement by the blood of Jesus
does not preach the cross! And he who does not declare justification by faith in Christ Jesus has missed the mark altogether.
This is the very heart of the Christian system. If our ministry shall
be without blood, it is without life, for *"the blood of it is for the
life thereof"* (Leviticus 17:14). He that preaches not justification
by faith knows not the doctrine of grace, for the Scripture says,
*"Therefore it is of faith, that it might be by grace; to the end the promise
might be sure to all the seed"* (Romans 4:16). Paul glories both in the
fact of the cross and in the doctrine of the cross.

3. THE CROSS OF THE DOCTRINE

The death of the Son of God upon the cross is the crux of
Christianity. Here is the difficulty, the stumbling block, the rock
of offense. The Jew could not endure a crucified Messiah—he
looked for pomp and power! Multitudinous ceremonies and different washings and sacrifices—were these all to be put away, and
nothing left but a bleeding Savior? At the mention of the cross,
the philosophic Greek thought himself insulted, and vilified the
preacher as a fool. In effect, he said, "You are not a man of thought
and intellect; you are not abreast of the times but are sticking in
the mire of antiquated prophecies. Why not advance with the discoveries of modern thought?" The apostle, teaching a simple fact
which a child might comprehend, found in it the wisdom of God!
Christ upon the cross, working out the salvation of men, was more
to him than all the sayings of the sages. As for the Roman, he
would give no heed to any glorying in a dead Jew, a crucified Jew!
Crushing the world beneath his iron heel, he declared that such
romancing would never win him from the gods of his fathers.

Paul did not budge before the sharp and practical reply of
the conquerors of the world! He did not tremble before Nero in
his palace. Whether to Greek or Jew, Roman or barbarian, bond

or free (see Galatians 3:28), he was not ashamed of the gospel of Christ (see Romans 1:16) but gloried in the cross. Though the testimony that the one all-sufficient atonement was provided on the cross stirs the enmity of man and provokes opposition, yet Paul was so far from attempting to mitigate that opposition that he determined to know nothing save for Jesus Christ and Him crucified! His motto was, *"We preach Christ crucified"* (1 Corinthians 1:23). He had the cross for his philosophy, the cross for his tradition, the cross for his gospel, the cross for his glory—and nothing else!

II. WHY DID PAUL GLORY IN THE CROSS?

1. FROM SOLEMN AND DELIBERATE CHOICE

He did not do so because he was in need of a theme, for, as I have shown you, he had a wide field for boasting if he had chosen to occupy it. He gloried in the cross from solemn and deliberate choice. He had counted the cost, he had surveyed the whole range of subjects with an eagle eye, and he knew what he did and why he did it. He was master of the art of thinking. As a metaphysician none could excel him. As a logical thinker none could have gone beyond him. He stands almost alone in the early Christian church as a mastermind. Others may have been more poetic, or simpler, but none was more thoughtful or argumentative than he. With decision and firmness, Paul set aside everything else and definitely declares, throughout his whole life, "I glory in the cross." He did this exclusively, saying, "God forbid that I should glory, save in the cross." There were many other precious things, but he put them all upon the shelf in comparison with the cross.

He would not even make his chief point any of the great scriptural doctrines, nor even an instructive and godly ordinance. No, the cross was to the front. This constellation was chief in Paul's sky. The choice of the cross he made devoutly, for although the expression used in our English version may not stand, yet I do not doubt that Paul would have used it and would have called upon God to witness that he abjured all other ground of glorying, save for the atoning Sacrifice:

Forbid it, Lord, that I should boast,
Save in the death of Christ, my God:
All the vain things that charm me most,
I sacrifice them to His blood.

He would have called God to witness that he knew no ambition save that of bringing glory to the cross of Christ. As I think of this, I am ready to say "Amen" to Paul and bid you sing that stirring verse:

It is the old cross still,
Hallelujah! Hallelujah!
Its triumphs let us tell,
Hallelujah! hallelujah!
The grace of God here shone
Through Christ, the blessed Son,
Who did for sin atone;
Hallelujah for the cross!

2. THE CROSS—AND THE ATONEMENT— IS THE CRUX OF CHRISTIANITY

Why did Paul thus glory in the cross? You may well desire to know, for there are many nowadays who do not glory in it but forsake it! Alas that it should be so, but there are ministers who ignore the atonement! They conceal the cross or say but little about it. You may go through service after service and scarcely hear a mention of the atoning blood. but Paul was always bringing forward the expiation for sin—he never tried to explain it away. Oh, the number of books that have been written to prove that the cross means an example of self-sacrifice, as if every martyrdom did not mean that! They cannot endure a real substitutionary Sacrifice for human guilt and an effectual purifying of sin by the death of the great Substitute. Yet the cross means that or nothing!

Paul was very bold. Although he knew this would make him many enemies, you never find him refining and spiritualizing; the cross and the atonement for sin were plain matters of fact to him. Neither did he attempt to decorate it by adding philosophical theories. No, to him it was the bare, naked cross, all blood-stained and despised! In this he gloried and in none of the wisdom of words with which others vexed him. He would have the cross—the cross and nothing but the cross! He pronounced an anathema on all who proposed a rival theme: *"But though we, or an angel from heaven, preach any other gospel unto you than that which we have preached to you, let him be accursed"* (Galatians 1:8).

I take it that this was so, first, because Paul saw in the cross a vindication of divine justice. Where else can the justice of God be seen so clearly as in the death of God Himself in the person of His dear Son? If the Lord Himself suffers on account of broken law, then is the majesty of the law honored to the fullest! Some time ago, a judge in America was called upon to try a prisoner who had been his companion in his early youth. It was a crime for which the penalty was a fine, more or less heavy. The judge did not diminish the fine. The case was clearly a bad one, and he fined the prisoner the maximum fine. Some who knew his former relation to the offender thought him somewhat unkind to thus carry out the law, while others admired his impartiality. All were surprised when the judge quit the bench and paid every farthing of the penalty! He had shown both his respect for the law and his goodwill to the man who had broken it. He exacted the penalty, but he paid it himself.

So, God has done in the person of His dear Son. He has not remitted the punishment, but He has Himself endured it. His own Son, who is none other than God Himself—for there is an essential union between them—has paid the debt which was incurred by human sin. I love to think of the vindication of divine justice upon the cross. I am never weary of it! Some cannot bear the thought, but to me it seems inevitable that sin must be punished, or else the foundations of society would be removed. If sin becomes a trifle, virtue will be a toy! Society cannot stand if laws are left without penal sanction, or if that sanction is to be a mere empty threat. Men in their own governments, every now and then, cry out for greater severity. When a certain offense abounds, and ordinary means fail, they demand exemplary punishment—and it is but natural that they should do so, for deep in the conscience of every man there is the conviction that sin must be punished to secure the general good. Justice must reign—even benevolence demands it! If there could have been salvation without an atonement, it would have been a calamity—righteous men, and even benevolent men, might deprecate the setting aside of law in order to save the guilty from the natural result of their crimes.

For my own part, I value a just salvation. An unjust salvation would never have satisfied the apprehensions and demands of my conscience. No, let God be just, even if the heavens fall! Let God carry out the sentence of His law, or the universe will suspect that it was not righteous—and when such a suspicion rules the general mind, all respect for God will be gone! The Lord carries out the decree of His justice even to the bitter end, abating not a jot of its requirements. Brothers and sisters, there was an infinite efficacy in the death of such a One as our Lord Jesus Christ to vindicate the law. Though He is Man, yet is He also God, and in His passion and death, He offered to the justice of God a vindication not at all inferior to the punishment of hell! God is just, indeed, when Jesus dies upon the cross rather than that God's law should be dishonored. When our august Lord Himself bore the wrath that was due for human sin, it was made evident to all that law is not to be trifled with. We glory in the cross, for there the debt was paid, our sins on Jesus laid.

But we glory because on the cross we have an unexampled display of God's love. *"God commends His love toward us, in that, while we were yet sinners, Christ died for us"* (Romans 5:8). Oh, to think of it—that He who was offended takes the nature of the offender and then bears the penalty due for wanton transgression! He who is infinite, thrice holy, all glorious, forever to be worshipped, yet stoops to be numbered with the transgressors and to bear the sin of many! The mythology of the gods of high Olympus contains nothing worthy to be mentioned in the same day with this wondrous deed of supreme condescension and infinite love! The ancient shastras and Vedas have nothing of the kind! The death of Jesus Christ upon the cross cannot be an invention of men—none of the ages have produced anything like it in the poetic dreams of any nation! If we did not hear of it so often and think of it so little, we would be charmed with it beyond expression! If we now heard of it for the first time and seriously believed it, I know not what we would not do in our glad surprise! Certainly, we would fall down and worship the Lord Jesus and continue to worship Him forever and ever!

3. THE CROSS REMOVES ALL GUILT

I believe again, third, that Paul delighted to preach the cross of Christ as the removal of all guilt. He believed that the Lord Jesus on the cross finished transgression, made an end of sin, and brought in everlasting righteousness. He that believes in Jesus is justified from all things from which he could not be justified by the law of Moses. Since sin was laid on Jesus, God's justice cannot lay it upon the believing sinner. The Lord will never punish the same offense twice. If He accepts a Substitute for me, how can He call me to His bar and punish me for that transgression for which my Substitute endured the chastisement? Many a troubled conscience has caught at this and found deliverance from despair. Wonder not that Paul gloried in Christ, since it is written, "*In the* LORD *shall all the seed of Israel be justified, and shall glory*" (Isaiah 45:25). This is the method of salvation which completely and eternally absolves the sinner and makes the blackest offender white as snow! Transgression visited upon Christ has ceased to be, so far as the believer is concerned. Does not faith cry, "You will cast all their sins into the depths of the sea"? O sirs, there is something to glory in in this, and those who know the sin-removing power of the cross will not be hindered in this glorying by all the powers of earth or hell!

4. THE CROSS IS THE PERFECTION OF WISDOM

Paul gloried in it, again, as a marvel of wisdom. It seemed to him the sum of perfect wisdom and skill. He cried, "*O the depth of the riches both of the wisdom and knowledge of God!*" (Romans 11:33). The plan of salvation by vicarious suffering is simple but sublime. It would have been impossible for human or angelic wisdom to have invented it! Men already so hate it and fight against it that they never would have devised it! God alone, out of the treasury of His infinite wisdom, brought forth this matchless project of salvation for the guilty through the substitution of the innocent. The more we study it, the more we shall perceive that it is full of teaching. It is only the superficial thinker who regards the cross as a subject soon to be comprehended and exhausted! The loftiest intellects will here find ample room and space enough. The most profound minds might lose themselves in considering the splendid diversities of light which compose the pure white light of the cross! Everything of sin and justice, of misery and mercy, of folly and wisdom, of force and tenderness, of rage and pity on the part of man and God may be seen here. In the cross may be seen the concentration of eternal thought, the focus of infinite purpose, the outcome of illimitable wisdom. Of God and the cross, we may say:

Here I behold His inmost heart,
Where grace and vengeance strangely join;
Piercing His Son with sharpest smart
To make the purchased pleasures mine.

5. THE CROSS IS THE DOOR OF HOPE FOR ALL

I believe that Paul gloried in the cross, again, because it is the door of hope even to the vilest of the vile. The world was very filthy in Paul's time. Roman civilization was of the most brutal and debased kind, and the masses of the people were sunken in vices that are altogether unmentionable. Paul felt that he could go into the darkest places with light in his hand when he spoke of the cross. To tell of pardon bought with the blood of the Son of God is to carry an omnipotent message! The cross lifts up the fallen and delivers the despairing. Today, my brothers and sisters, the world's one and only remedy is the cross. Go, you thinkers, and get up a mission to the fallen in London, leaving out the cross! Go now, you wise men, reclaim the harlots and win to virtue the degraded by your perfumed philosophies! See what you can do in the slums and alleys without the cross of Christ! Go talk to your titled reprobates and win them from their abominations by displays of art! You will fail, the most cultivated of you, even to win the rich and educated to anything like purity, unless your themes are drawn from Calvary and the love which there poured out its heart's blood!

This hammer breaks rocky hearts, but no other will do it. Pity itself stands silent. Compassion bites her lip and inwardly groans; she has nothing to say till she has learned the story of the cross. But with that on her tongue, she waxes eloquently! With tears she entreats, persuades, prevails! She may but stammer in her speech—like Moses, she may be slow of utterance (see Exodus 4:10)—but the cross is in her hand as the rod of the prophet. With this she conquers the pharaoh of tyrannical sin! With this she divides the Red Sea of guilt! With this she leads the host of God out of the house of bondage into the land of promise which flows with milk and honey! (See Exodus 3:17.) The cross is the standard of victorious grace! It is the lighthouse whose cheering ray gleams across the dark waters of despair and cheers the dense midnight of our fallen race, saving from eternal shipwreck and piloting into everlasting peace.

6. IT WAS A SOURCE OF REST

Again, Paul, I believe, gloried in the cross, as I often do, because it was the source of rest to him and to his brethren. I make this confession, and I make it very boldly, that I never knew what rest of heart truly meant till I understood the doctrine of the substitution of our Lord Jesus Christ. Now, when I see my Lord bearing away my sins as my Scapegoat, or dying for them as my Sin Offering, I feel a profound peace of heart and satisfaction of spirit. The cross is all I ever need for security and joy. Truly, this bed is long enough for a man to stretch himself on. The cross is a chariot of salvation where we traverse the high road of life without fear! The pillow of atonement heals the head that aches with anguish. Beneath the shadow of the cross, I sit down with great delight, and its fruit is sweet to my taste. I have no impatience even to hasten to heaven while resting beneath the cross, for our hymn truly says:

Here it is I find my heaven,
While upon the cross I gaze.

Here is perfect cleansing and, therefore, a divine security guarded by the justice of God. Here is, therefore, a *"peace of God, which passes all understanding"* (Philippians 4:7). To try to entice me away from the God's truth of substitution is labor in vain! Seduce me to preach the pretty nothings of modern thought? This child knows much better than to leave the substance for the shadow, the truth for the fancy! I see nothing that can give to my heart a fair exchange for the rest, peace, and unutterable joy which the old-fashioned doctrine of the cross now yields me. Will a man leave bread for husks and quit the home of his love to dwell in a desolate wilderness? I dare not renounce the truth of God in order to be thought cultured! I am no more a fool than the most of my contemporaries, and if I could see anything better than the cross, I would willingly grasp it as they—for it is a flattering thing to be thought a man of light and leading! But where shall I go if I quit the Rock of the atoning sacrifice? I cannot go beyond my simple faith that Jesus stood in my place and bore my sin and took it away. This I must preach! I know nothing else! God help me, I will never go an inch beyond the cross, for to me all else is vanity and vexation of spirit! Return unto your rest, O my soul! Where else is there a glimpse of hope for you but in Him who loved you and gave Himself for you?

7. HE SAW IT AS THE SOURCE OF ENTHUSIASM

I am sure Paul gloried in the cross yet, again, because he saw it to be the creator of enthusiasm. Christianity finds its chief force in the enthusiasm which the Holy Spirit produces—and this comes from the cross. The preaching of the cross is the great weapon of the crusade against evil. In the old times, vast crowds came together in desert places, among the hills, or on the moors, at peril of their lives, to hear preaching. Did they come together to hear philosophy? Did they meet in the dead of night, when the hounds of persecution were hunting them, to listen to pretty moral essays? I think not! They came to hear of the grace of God manifest in the sacrifice of Jesus to believing hearts! Would your modern gospel create the spirit of the martyrs? Is there anything in it for which a man might go to prison and to death? The modern speculations are not worth a cat's dying for them, much less a man!

Something lies within the truth of the cross which sets the soul aglow! It touches the preacher's lips as with a live coal and fires the hearers' hearts as with flame from the altar of God. We can live on this gospel—and for this gospel die. Atonement by blood, full deliverance from sin, perfect safety in Christ given to the believer—these call a man to joy, to gratitude, to consecration, to decision, to patience, to holy living, to all-consuming zeal! Therefore, in the doctrine of the cross we glory. Neither will we be slow to speak it out with all our might!

III. WHAT WAS THE CROSS'S EFFECT UPON PAUL?

The cross is never without influence. Come where it may, it works for life or for death. Wherever there is Christ's cross, there are also two other crosses. On either side there is one, and Jesus is in the middle. Two thieves are crucified with Christ, and Paul tells us their names in his case: "*The world is crucified to me, and I to the world*" (Galatians 6:14.) Self and the world are both crucified when Christ's cross appears and is believed in!

1. SELF AND THE WORLD WERE CRUCIFIED TO HIM

Beloved, what does Paul mean? Does he not mean just this—that ever since he had seen Christ, he looked upon the world as a crucified, hung-up thing which had no more power over him than a criminal hanged upon a cross? What power has a corpse on a gallows? Such power had the world over Paul. The world despised him, and he could not go after the world if he would—and would not go after it if he could! He was dead to it, and it was dead to him; therefore, there was a double separation!

How does the cross do this? To be under the dominion of this present evil world is horrible—how does the cross help us to escape? Why, brothers and sisters, he that has ever seen the cross looks upon the world's pomp and glory as a vain show! The pride of heraldry and the glitter of honor fade into meanness before the Crucified One. O you great ones, what are your silks, your furs, your jewelry, your gold, your stars, and your garters to one who has learned to glory in Christ crucified? The old clothes which belong to the hangman are quite as precious. The world's light is darkness when the Sun of Righteousness shines from the cross! What do we care for all the kingdoms of the world and the glory thereof when once we see the thorn-crowned Lord? There is more glory about one nail of the cross than about all the scepters of all kings! Let the knights of the Golden Fleece meet in chapter and all the knights of the Garter stand in their stalls, but what is all their splendor? Their glories wither before the inevitable hour of doom, while the glory of the cross is eternal! Everything of earth grows dull and dim when seen by the light of the cross!

So was it with the world's approval. Paul would not ask the world to be pleased with him, since it knew not his Lord, or only knew Him to crucify Him. Can a Christian be ambitious to be written down as one of the world's foremost men when that world cast out his Lord? They crucified our Master! Shall His servants court their love? Such approval would be all stained with blood. They crucified my Master, the Lord of glory—do I want them to smile on me and say to me, "Reverend Sir," or, "Learned Doctor"? No! The friendship of the world is enmity with God and, therefore, to be dreaded! (See James 4:4.) Mouths that spit on Jesus shall give me no kisses! Those who hate the doctrine of the atonement hate my life and soul—and I desire not their esteem.

Paul also saw that the world's wisdom was absurd. That age talked of being wise and philosophical! Yes, and its philosophy brought it to crucify the Lord of glory! It did not know perfection nor perceive the beauty of pure unselfishness. To slay the Messiah was the outcome of the culture of the Pharisee. To put to death the greatest Teacher of all time was the ripe fruit of Sadducean thought. The serious thoughts of the present age have performed no greater feat than to deny the doctrine of satisfaction for sin! They have crucified our Lord afresh by their criticisms and their new theologies—and this is all the world's wisdom ever does. Its wisdom lies in scattering doubt, quenching hope, and denying certainty—and, therefore, the wisdom of the world to us is sheer folly! (See 1 Corinthians 3:18–20.) This century's philosophy will one day be spoken of as an evidence that softening of the brain was very usual among its scientific men! We count the thought of the present moment to be methodical madness, bedlam out of doors, and those who are furthest gone in it are credulous beyond imagination! God has poured contempt upon the wise men of this world! Their foolish heart is blinded; they grope at noonday. (See Deuteronomy 28:28–29.)

2. HE SAW WORLDLY TRAPPINGS AS NOTHING

So, too, the apostle Paul saw the world's religion to be nothing. It was the world's religion that crucified Christ. The priests were at the bottom of it; the Pharisees urged it on. The church of the nation, the church of many ceremonies, the church which loved the traditions of the elders, the church of phylacteries and broad-bordered garments—it was this church, which, acting by its officers, crucified the Lord! Paul therefore looked with pity upon priests and altars and upon all the attempts of a Christless world to make up, by finery of worship, for the absence of the Spirit of God. Once see Christ on the cross, and architecture and fine display become gaudy, cheap things. The cross calls for worship in spirit and in truth—and the world knows nothing of this.

And so it was with the world's pursuits. Some ran after honor, some toiled after learning, others labored for riches. But to Paul, these were all trifles since he had seen Christ on the cross. He that has seen Jesus die will never go into the toy business—he puts away childish things. A child, a pipe, a little soap, and many pretty bubbles—such is the world. The cross alone can wean us from such play.

And so it was with the world's pleasures and with the world's power. The world, and everything that belonged to the world, had become as a corpse to Paul, and he was as a corpse to it. See where the corpse swings in chains on the gallows. What a foul, rotten thing! We cannot endure it! Do not let it hang longer above ground to fill the air with pestilence. Let the dead be buried out of sight. The Christ that died upon the cross now lives in our hearts. The Christ that took human guilt has taken possession of our souls, and therefore we live only in Him, for Him, by Him. He has engrossed our affections. All our ardors burn for Him. God make it to be so with us, that we may glorify God and bless our age!

Paul concludes this epistle by saying, *"From hereafter let no man trouble me: for I bear in my body the marks of the* LORD *Jesus"* (Galatians 6:17). He was a slave, branded with his Master's name. That stamp could never be erased, for it was burned into his heart. Even thus, I trust the doctrine of the atonement is our settled belief, and faith in it is part of our life. We are rooted and grounded in the unchanging truths of God! Do not try to convert me to your new views—I am past it. Forget about me! You waste your breath. It is done—on this point the wax takes no farther impress. I have taken up my standing and will never quit it. A crucified Christ has taken such possession of my entire nature—spirit, soul, and body—that I am henceforth beyond the reach of opposing arguments!

Brothers and sisters, will you enlist under the conquering banner of the cross? Once rolled in the dust and stained in blood, it now leads on the armies of the Lord to victory! Oh, that all ministers would preach the true doctrine of the cross! Oh, that all Christian people would live under the influence of it, and we should then see brighter days than these! Unto the Crucified be glory forever and ever! Amen.

IO

THE STONE ROLLED AWAY

"The angel of the LORD descended from heaven, and came and rolled back the stone from the door, and sat upon it."
—Matthew 28:2

As the holy women went toward the sepulcher in the twilight of the morning, desirous to embalm the body of Jesus (see Matthew 28:1), they recollected that the huge stone at the door of the tomb would be a great impediment in their way, and they said one to another, *"Who shall roll away the stone...?"* (Mark 16:3). That question gathers up the mournful enquiry of the whole universe. They seem to have put into language the great sigh of universal manhood: "Who shall roll away the stone?" In man's path of happiness lies a huge rock which completely blocks the road. Who among the mighty shall remove the barrier? Philosophy attempted the task but miserably failed. In the ascent to immortality, the stone of doubt, uncertainty, and unbelief stopped all progress. Who could remove the awful mass and bring life and immortality to light?

Men, generation after generation, buried their fellows—the all-devouring sepulcher swallowed its myriads. Who could stop the daily slaughter or give a hope beyond the grave? There was a whisper of resurrection, but men could not believe in it. Some dreamed of a future state and talked of it in mysterious poetry, as though it were all imagination and nothing more. In darkness and in twilight, with many fears and few guesses at the truth, men continued to enquire, "Who shall roll away the stone?"

Men had an indistinct feeling that this worm could not be all—that there must be another life, that intelligent creatures could not all have come into this world that they might perish. It was hoped, at any rate, that there was something beyond the fatal river. It scarcely could be that none returned from Avernus—there surely must be a way out of the sepulcher. Difficult as the pathway might be, men hoped that surely there must be some return from the land of death shade, and the question was therefore ever rising to the heart, if not to the lips: "Where is the coming man? Where is the predestinated deliverer? Where is he, and who is he, that shall roll away the stone?"

To the women there were three difficulties. The stone itself was huge. It was stamped with the seal of the law. It was guarded by the representatives of power. To mankind there were the same three difficulties. Death itself was a huge stone not to be moved by any strength known to mortals. That death was evidently sent of God as a penalty for offenses against His law—how could it therefore be averted? How could it be removed? The red seal of God's vengeance was set upon that sepulcher's mouth—how should that seal be broken? Who could roll the stone away?

Moreover, demon forces and powers of hell were watching the sepulcher to prevent escape—who could encounter these and bear departed souls like a prey from between the lion's teeth? It was a dreary question, "Who shall roll away the stone from the sepulcher?" "Can these dry bones live? (See Ezekiel 37:3.) Shall our departed ones be restored to us? Can the multitudes of our race who have gone down to Hades ever return from the land of midnight and confusion?" So asked all heathendom, "Who?" And echo answered, "Who?"

No answer was given to sages and kings, but the women who loved the Savior found an answer! They came to the tomb of Christ, but it was empty, for Jesus had risen! (See Mark 16:4–6.) Here is the answer to the world's enquiry—there is another life! Bodies will live again, for Jesus lives! O mourning Rachel, refusing to be comforted, *"Refrain your voice from weeping, and your eyes from tears: for your work shall be rewarded,…and they shall come again from the land of the enemy"* (Jeremiah 31:16). Sorrow no longer, you mourners, around the grave, as those that are without hope—for since Jesus Christ is risen, the dead in Christ shall rise also! (See 1 Thessalonians 4:16.)

Wipe away those tears, for the believer's grave is no longer the place for lamentations—it is but the passage to immortality! It is but the dressing room in which the spirit shall put aside, for a while, her travel-worn garments of her earthly journey—to put them on again on a brighter morrow, when they shall be fair and white as no launderer on earth could make them!

I purpose this morning to talk a little concerning the resurrection of our exalted Lord Jesus, and, that the subject may the more readily interest you, I shall first of all bid this stone which was rolled away preach to you. And then I shall invite you to hear the angel's homily from his pulpit of stone.

I. LET THE STONE PREACH

It is not at all an uncommon thing to find in Scripture stones bid to speak. (See, for example, Luke 19:40.) Great stones have been rolled as witnesses against the people. Stones and beams out of the wall have been called upon to testify to sin. I shall call this stone as a witness to valuable truths of God of which it was the symbol. The river of our thought divides into six streams.

I. THE STONE AS DOOR OF THE SEPULCHER

The stone rolled must evidently be regarded as the door of the sepulcher removed. Death's house was firmly secured by a huge stone. The angel removed it, and the living Christ came forth. (See Matthew 28:2.) The massive door, you will observe, was taken away from the grave—not merely opened but unhinged, flung aside, rolled away! And now death's ancient prison is without a door! The saints shall pass in, but they shall not be shut in. They shall tarry there as in an open cavern, but there is nothing to prevent their coming forth from it in due time.

As Samson, when he slept in Gaza and was beset by foes, arose early in the morning and took upon his shoulders the gates of Gaza—posts and bars and all—and carried all away and left the Philistine stronghold open and exposed (see Judges 16:3), so has it been done unto the grave by our Master, who, having slept out His three days and nights, according to the divine decree (see Luke 24:46), arose in the greatness of His strength and bore away the iron gates of the sepulcher, tearing every bar from its place. The removal of the imprisoning stone was the outward type of our Lord's having plucked up the gates of the grave—posts, bars, and all—thus exposing that old fortress of death and hell and leaving it as a city stormed and taken and bereft of power.

Remember that our Lord was committed to the grave as a hostage. He died for our sins. (See 1 Corinthians 15:3.) Like a debt they were imputed to Him. He discharged the debt of obligation due from us to God on the cross—He suffered to the full the great substitutionary equivalent for our suffering, and then He was confined in the tomb as a hostage until His work should be fully accepted. That acceptance would be notified by His coming forth from vile durance. And that coming forth would become our justification! He rose again for our justification. (See Romans 4:25.) If He had not fully paid the debt,

He would have remained in the grave. If Jesus had not made effectual, total, final atonement, He would have continued as a captive.

But He had done it all. *"It is finished"* (John 19:30), which came from His own lips, was established by the verdict of Jehovah, and Jesus was set free. Mark Him as He rises—not breaking out of prison like a felon who escapes from justice but coming leisurely forth like one whose time of release from jail is come. Rising, it is true, by His own power, but not leaving the tomb without a sacred permit—the heavenly officer from the court of heaven is deputized to open the door for Him by rolling away the stone. And Jesus Christ, completely justified, rises to prove that all His people are, in Him, completely justified, and the work of salvation is forever perfect!

The stone is rolled from the door of the sepulcher as if to show that Jesus has so effectually done the work that nothing can shut us up in the grave again. The grave has changed its character. It has been altogether annihilated and put away as a prison, so that death to the saints is no longer a punishment for sin but an entrance into rest! Come, brethren, let us rejoice in this! In the empty tomb of Christ, we see sin forever put away—we see, therefore, death most effectually destroyed! Our sins were the great stone which shut the mouth of the sepulcher and held us captives in death and darkness and despair. Our sins are now forever rolled away, and therefore death is no longer a dungeon, dark and drear, the antechamber of hell, but rather it is a perfumed bedchamber, a withdrawing room, the vestibule of heaven!

As surely as Jesus rose, so must His people leave the dead—there is nothing to prevent the resurrection of the saints. The stone which could keep us in the prison has been rolled away! Who can bar us in when the door itself is gone? Who can confine us when every barricade is taken away?

Who shall rebuild for the tyrant his prison?
The scepter lies broken that fell from his hands!
The stone is removed. The Lord is risen!
The helpless shall soon be released from their bands.

2. THE STONE AS A MEMORIAL TROPHY

Regard the stone as a trophy, set up. As men of old set up memorial stones, and as at this day we erect columns to tell of great deeds of prowess, so that stone rolled away was, as it were, before the eyes of our faith consecrated that day as a memorial of Christ's eternal victory over the powers of death and hell. They thought that they had vanquished Him. They deemed that the Crucified was overcome. Grimly did they smile as they saw His motionless body wrapped in the winding-sheet and put away in Joseph's new tomb. But their joy was fleeting! Their boasting was but brief, for at the appointed moment He who could not see corruption rose and came forth from beneath their power! His heel was bruised by the old serpent, but on the resurrection morning He crushed the dragon's head:

Vain the stone, the watch, the seal,
Christ has burst the gates of Hell!
Death in vain forbids His rise,
Christ has opened Paradise!
Lives again our glorious King!
"Where, O Death, is now your sting?"
Once He died our souls to save—
"Where's your victory, boasting grave?"

Brethren beloved in Christ, as we look at yonder stone, with the angel seated upon it, it rises before us as a monument of Christ's victory over death and hell. It becomes us to remember that His victory was achieved for us and that the fruits of it are all ours! We have to fight with sin, but Christ has overcome it! We are tempted by Satan—Christ has given Satan a defeat. We by and by shall leave this body unless the Lord comes speedily. We may expect to gather up our feet like our fathers and go to meet our God. But death is vanquished for us, and we can have no cause to fear! Courage, Christian soldiers, you are encountering a vanquished enemy!

Remember that the Lord's victory is a guarantee for yours! If the Head conquers, the members shall not be defeated. Let not sorrow dim your eyes, let no fears trouble your spirit—you must conquer, for Christ has conquered! Awaken all your powers to the conflict and nerve them with the hope of victory. Had you seen your Master defeated, you might expect yourself to be blown like chaff before the wind. But the power by which He overcame He lends to you! The Holy Spirit is in you! Jesus Himself has promised to be with you always, even to the end of the world (see Matthew 28:20), and the mighty God is your Refuge. You shall surely overcome through the blood of the Lamb! (See Revelation 12:11.) Set up that stone before your faith's eye this morning and say, "Here my Master conquered hell and death, and in His name and by His strength I shall be crowned, too, when the last enemy is destroyed."

3. THE STONE AS A FOUNDATION LAID FOR FAITH

Observe that here is a foundation laid. That stone rolled away from the sepulcher, typifying and certifying, as it does, the resurrection of Jesus Christ, is a foundation stone for Christian faith. The fact of the resurrection is the keystone of Christianity. Disprove the resurrection of our Lord, and our holy faith would be a mere fable! There would be nothing for faith to rest upon if He who died upon the cross did not also rise again from the tomb! Then, in the words of the apostle Paul, *"your faith is vain; you are yet in your sins...[while] they also which are fallen asleep in Christ are perished"* (1 Corinthians 15:17–18).

All the great doctrines of our divine religion fall asunder like the stones of an arch when the keystone is dislodged—in a common ruin they are all overthrown, for all our hope hinges upon that great fact. If Jesus rose, then is this gospel what it professes to be! If He rose not from the dead, then is it all deceit and delusion! But, brothers and sisters, that Jesus rose from the dead is a fact better established than almost any other in history. The witnesses were many—they were men of all classes and conditions. None of them ever confessed himself mistaken or deceived. They were so persuaded that it was a fact that the most of them suffered death for bearing witness to it!

They had nothing to gain by such a witness! They did not rise in power nor gain honor or wealth. They were truthful, simple-minded men who testified what they had seen and bore witness to that which they had beheld. The resurrection is a fact better attested than any event recorded in history, whether ancient or modern. Here is the confidence of the saints—our Lord Jesus Christ, who witnessed a good confession before Pontius Pilate and was crucified, dead, and buried, rose again from the dead, and after forty days ascended to the throne of God.

We rest in Him! We believe in Him! If He had not risen, we had been of all men most miserable to have been His followers. If He had not risen, His atonement would not have been proved sufficient. If He had not risen, His blood would not have been proven to us to be efficacious for the taking away of sin! But as He has risen, we build upon this truth of God—all our confidence we rest upon it, and we are persuaded that…

Raised from the dead, He goes before;
He opens Heaven's eternal door;
To give His saints a blest abode,
Near their Redeemer and their God.

My dear hearers, are you resting your everlasting hopes upon the resurrection of Jesus Christ from the dead? Do you trust in Him, believing that He both died and rose again for you? Do you place your entire dependence upon the merit of His blood, certified by the fact of His rising again? If so, you have a foundation of fact and truth—a foundation against which the gates of hell shall not prevail! But if you are building upon anything that you have done or anything that priestly hands can do for you, you are building upon the sands which shall be swept away by the all-devouring flood, and you and your hopes, too, shall go down into the fathomless abyss wrapped in the darkness of despair! Oh, to build upon the living Stone of Christ Jesus! Oh, to rest on Him who is a tried Cornerstone, elect, precious! This is to build safely, eternally, and blessedly!

4. THE STONE AS A PLACE OF REST

The angel seemed to teach us, as he sat down upon the stone, that the stone provided a place of rest. (See Matthew 28:2.) How leisurely the whole resurrection was effected! How noiselessly, too! What an absence of pomp and parade! The angel descended. The stone was rolled away. Christ rose, and then the angel sat down on the stone—he sat there silently and gracefully, breathing defiance to the Jews and to their seal, to the Roman legionaries and their spears, to death, to earth, to hell. He did as good as say, "Come and roll that stone back again, you enemies of the Risen One! All you infernal powers who thought to prevail against our ever-living Prince, roll back that stone again, if you dare or can!"

The angel said not this in words, but his stately and quiet sitting upon the stone meant all that and more. The Master's work is done, and done forever, and this stone, no more to be used—this unhinged door no more employed to shut in the tomb; it is the type of "it is finished": finished so as never to be undone, finished so as to last eternally! Yon resting angel softly whispers to us, "Come here and rest also." There is no fuller, better, surer, safer rest for the soul than in the fact that the Savior in whom we trust has risen from the dead! Do you mourn departed friends today? O come and sit upon this stone which tells you they shall rise again!

Do you expect to die soon? Is the worm at the root? Have you the flush of consumption on your cheek? O come and sit down upon this stone and remember that death has lost its terror now, for Jesus has risen from the tomb! Come, too, you feeble and trembling ones, and breathe defiance to death and hell. The angel will vacate his seat for you and let you sit down in the face of the enemy. Though you are but a humble woman, or a man broken down and pale and languid with long years of weary sickness, yet may you well defy all the hosts of hell while resting upon this precious truth of God: *"He is not here: for He is risen"* (Matthew 28:6). "He has left the dead, no more to die."

I was reminded, as I thought over this passage of my discourse, of that time when Jacob journeyed to the house of Laban. (See Genesis 27:41–46.) It is said he came to a place where there was a well, and a great stone lay upon it, and the flocks and herds were gathered round it, but they had no water till one came and rolled away the great stone from the well's mouth, and then they watered the flocks. (See Genesis 29.) Even so the tomb of Jesus is like a great well springing up with the purest and most divine refreshment— but until this stone was rolled away, none of the flocks redeemed by blood could be watered there! But now, every Sunday, on the resurrection morning, the first day of the week, we gather round our Lord's open sepulcher and draw living waters from that sacred well!

O you weary sheep of the fold, O you who are faint and ready to die, come here! Here is sweet refreshment! Jesus Christ is risen! Let your comforts be multiplied!

Every note with wonders swell,
Sin overthrown and captive hell;

Where is hell's once dreaded king?
Where, O Death, your mortal sting? Hallelujah.

5. THE STONE AS AN APPOINTED BOUNDARY

Do you not see it so? Behold it, then—there it lies, and the angel sits upon it. On that side what do you see? The guards frightened, stiffened with fear, like dead men. On this side what do you see? The timid, trembling women, to whom the angel softly speaks: *"Fear not you: for I know that you seek Jesus"* (Matthew 28:5). You see, then, that stone became the boundary between the living and the dead, between the seekers and the haters, between the friends and the foes of Christ. To His enemies, His resurrection is *"a stone of stumbling, and a rock of offense"* (1 Peter 2:8). As of old on Mar's Hill, when the sages heard of the resurrection, they mocked. But to His own people, the resurrection is the headstone of the corner.

Our Lord's resurrection is our triumph and delight! The resurrection acts much in the same manner as the pillar which Jehovah placed between Israel and Egypt—it was darkness to Egypt, but it gave light to Israel! (See Exodus 14:19–20.) All was dark amidst Egypt's hosts, but all was brightness and comfort among Israel's tribes! So the resurrection is a doctrine full of horror to those who know not Christ and trust Him not. What have they to gain by resurrection? Happy were they could they sleep in everlasting annihilation!

What have they to gain by Christ's resurrection? Shall He come whom they have despised? Is He living whom they have hated and abhorred? Will He bid them rise? Will they have to meet Him as a judge upon the throne? The very thought of this is enough to strike through the loins of kings! But what will the fact of it be when the clarion trumpet startles all the sons of Adam from their last beds of dust? Oh, the horrors of that tremendous morning, when every sinner shall rise, and the risen Savior shall come in the clouds of heaven, and all the holy angels with Him! (See 1 Thessalonians 4:16.) Truly, there is nothing but dismay for those who are on the evil side of that resurrection stone!

But how great the joy which the resurrection brings to those who are on the right side of that stone! How they look for His appearing with daily growing transport! How they build upon the sweet truth of God that they shall arise and with these eyes see their Savior! I would have you ask yourselves this morning on which side you are of that boundary stone. Have you life in Christ? Are you risen with Christ? Do you trust alone in Him who rose from the dead? If so, fear not! The angel comforts you, and Jesus cheers you! But oh, if you have no life in Christ but are dead while you live, let the very thought that Jesus is risen strike you with fear and make you tremble—for tremble well you may at that which awaits you.

6. THE STONE AS A FORESHADOW OF RUIN

Our Lord came into this world to destroy all the works of Satan. Behold before you the works of the devil pictured as a grim and horrible castle, massive and terrible, overgrown with the moss of ages, colossal, stupendous, cemented with blood of men, ramparted by mischief and craft, surrounded with deep trenches, and garrisoned with fiends—a structure dread enough to cause despair to everyone who goes round about it to count its towers and mark its bulwarks.

In the fullness of time our Champion came into the world to destroy the works of the devil. During His life He sounded an alarm at the great castle and dislodged here and there a stone— for the sick were healed, the dead were raised, and the poor had the gospel preached to them. But on the resurrection morning the huge fortress trembled from top to bottom! Huge rifts were in its walls, and tottering were all its strongholds! A stronger than the master of that citadel had evidently entered it and was beginning to overturn, overturn, overturn, from pinnacle to basement! One huge stone upon which the building much depended—a corner-stone which knit the whole fabric together—was lifted bodily from its bed and hurled to the ground. Jesus tore the huge granite stone of death from its position and so gave a sure token that every other would follow!

When that stone was rolled away from Jesus's sepulcher, it was a prophecy that every stone of Satan's building should come down, and not one should rest upon another of all that the powers of darkness had ever piled up—from the days of their first apostasy even unto the end! Brothers and sisters, that stone rolled away from the door of the sepulcher gives me glorious hope! Evil is still mighty, but evil will come down! Spiritual wickedness reigns in high places; the multitude still clamor after evil; the nations still sit in thick darkness. Many worship the scarlet woman of Babylon. (See Revelation 17:3–5.) Others bow before the crescent of Mohammed, and millions bend themselves before blocks of wood and stone. The dark places and habitations of the earth are still full of cruelty.

But Christ has given such a shiver to the whole fabric of evil that, depend upon it, every stone will be certain to fall. We have but to work on—use the battering ram of the gospel, continue each one to keep in his place, and, like the hosts around Jericho, sound the trumpet (see Joshua 6:1–20)—and the day must come when every hoary evil, every colossal superstition shall be laid low! And the prophecy shall be fulfilled, *"I will overturn, overturn, overturn, it: and it shall be no more, until He come whose right it is; and I will give it Him"* (Ezekiel 21:27).

That loosened stone on which the angel sits is the assurance of the coming doom of everything that is base and vile! Rejoice, you sons of God, for Babylon's fall draws near! Sing, O heavens, and rejoice, O earth, for there shall not an evil be spared. Verily, I say unto you, there shall not be one stone left upon another which shall not be cast down. Thus has the stone preached to us—we will pause awhile and hear what the angel has to say.

II. THE ANGEL PREACHED

The angel preached two ways: he preached in symbol and he preached in words. Preaching in symbol is very popular with a certain party nowadays. The gospel is to be seen by the eyes, they tell us, and the people are to learn from the change of colors, at various seasons, such as blue and green and violet—exhibited on the priest and the altar, and by lace, and by candles, and by banners, and by cruets, and shells full of water! They are even to be taught or led by the nose, which is to be indulged with smoke of incense, and drawn by the ears, which are to listen to hideous chants or to dainty canticles.

Now, mark well that the angel was a symbolical preacher with his brow of lightning and his robe of snow! But you will please to notice for whom the symbols were reserved. He did not say a word to the keepers—not a word. He gave them the symbolic gospel, that is to say, he looked upon them—and his glance was lightning! He revealed himself to them in his snow-white garments and no more. Mark how they quake and tremble! That is the gospel of symbols, and wherever it comes it condemns.

It can do no other. Why, the old Mosaic law of symbols, where did it end? How few ever reached its inner meaning! The mass of Israel fell into idolatry, and the symbolic system became death to them. You who delight in symbols; you who think it is Christian to make the whole year a kind of practical charade upon the life of Christ; you who think that all Christianity is to be taught in semi-dramas, as men perform in theaters and puppet shows—go your way, for you shall meet no heaven on that road: no Christ, no life! You shall meet with priests, and formalists, and hypocrites, and into the thick woods and among the dark mountains of destruction shall you stumble to your utter ruin!

The gospel message is this: *"Incline your ear, and come to Me: hear, and your soul shall live"* (Isaiah 55:3). This is the life-giving message: *"Believe on the LORD Jesus Christ, and you shall be saved"* (Acts 16:31). But oh, perverse generation! If you look for symbols and signs, you shall be deluded with the devil's gospel and fall a prey to the destroyer! Now we will listen to the angel's sermon in words. Thus, only is a true gospel to be delivered. Christ is the Word, and the gospel is a gospel of words and thoughts. It does not appeal to the eyes—it appeals to the ears and to the intellect and to the heart. It is a spiritual thing and can only be learned by those whose spirits are awakened to grasp at the spiritual truths of God.

The first thing the angel said was, *"Fear not"* (Matthew 28:5). Oh, this is the very genius of our risen Savior's gospel: *"Fear not."* You who would be saved, you who would follow Christ—you need not fear! Did the earth quake? Fear not! God can preserve you though the earth is burned with fire! Did the angel descend in terrors? Fear not! There are no terrors in heaven for the child of God who comes to Jesus's cross and trusts his soul to Him who bled there. Poor women, is it the dark that alarms you? Fear not! God sees and loves you in the dark, and there is nothing in the dark or in the light beyond His control. (See Psalm 139:11–12.)

Are you afraid to come to a tomb? Does a sepulcher alarm you? Fear not! You cannot die. Since Christ has risen, though you were dead, yet should you live. (See John 11:25.) Oh, the comfort of the gospel! Permit me to say there is nothing in the Bible to make any man fear who puts his trust in Jesus. Nothing in the Bible, did I say? There is nothing in heaven, nothing on earth, nothing in hell that need make you fear who trust in Jesus. *"Fear not."* The past you need not fear—it is forgiven you. The present you need not fear—it is provided for. The future, also, is secured by the living power of Jesus. He says, *"Because I live, you shall live also"* (John 14:19).

Fear? Why, that were comely and seemly when Christ was dead, but now that He lives there remains no space for it! Do you fear your sins? They are all gone, for Christ had not risen if He had not put them all away! What is it you fear? If an angel bids you, *"Fear not,"* why will you fear? If every wound of the risen Savior and every act of your reigning Lord consoles you, why are you still dismayed? To be doubting and fearing and trembling, now that Jesus has risen, is an inconsistent thing in any believer! Jesus is able to succor you in all your temptations, seeing He ever lives to make intercession for you; He is able to save you to the uttermost—therefore, do not fear! (See Hebrews 7:25.)

Notice the next word spoken by the angel: *"Fear not you: for I know…"* (Matthew 28:5). What? Does an angel know the women's hearts? Did the angel know what Mary Magdalene was about? Do spirits read our spirits? 'Tis well. But oh, 'tis better to remember that our heavenly Father knows. Fear not, for God knows what is in your heart. You have never made an avowal of anxiety about your soul; you are too bashful even for that—you have not even proceeded so far as to dare to say that you hope you love Jesus—but God knows your desires.

Poor heart, you feel as if you could not trust and could not do anything that is good! But you do at least desire, you do at least seek. All this God knows. With pleasure He spies out your desires. Does not this comfort you—this great fact of the knowledge of God? I could not read what is in your spirit, and perhaps you could not tell me what is there. If you tried, you would say, after you had done, "Well, I did not tell him exactly what I felt. I have missed the comfort I might have had, for I did not explain my case." But there is One who deals with you and knows exactly where your difficulty is and what is the cause of your present sorrow. *"Fear not,"* for your heavenly Father knows! Lie still, poor patient, for the Surgeon knows where the wound is and what it is that ails you. Hush, my child, be still upon your great Parent's bosom, for He knows all. And ought not that content you—that His care is as infinite as His knowledge?

Then the angel went on to say, *"Fear not you: for I know that you seek Jesus, which was crucified"* (Matthew 28:5). There was room for comfort here. They were seeking Jesus, though the world had crucified Him. Though the many had turned aside and left Him, they were clinging to Him in loving loyalty.

Now, is there anyone here who can say, "Though I am unworthy to be a follower of Christ and often think that He will reject me, yet there is one thing I am sure of—I would not be afraid of the fear of man for His sake. My sins make me fear, but no man could do it. I would stand at His side if all the world were against Him. I would count it my highest honor that the Crucified One of the world should be the adored One of my heart. Let all the world cast Him out, if He would but take me in, poor, unworthy worm as I am, I would never be ashamed to own His blessed and gracious name"? Ah, then do not fear, for if that is how you feel toward Christ, He will own you in the Last Great Day. If you are willing to own Him now, *"Fear not."* I am sure I sometimes feel, when I am looking into my own heart, as if I had neither part nor lot in the matter and could claim no interest in the Beloved at all. But then, I do know this: I am not ashamed to be put to shame for Him—and if I should be charged with being a fanatic and an enthusiast in His cause, I would count it the highest honor to plead guilty to so blessed an impeachment for His dear sake.

If this is truly the language of our hearts, we may take courage. *"Fear not you: for I know that you seek Jesus, which was crucified"* (Matthew 28:5). Then he adds, *"He is not here: for He is risen"* (Matthew 28:6). Here is the instruction which the angel gives. After giving comfort, he gives instruction. Your great ground and reason for consolation, seeker, is that you do not seek a dead Christ, and you do not pray to a buried Savior! He is really alive! Today He is as able to relieve you, if you go to your closet and pray to Him, as He was to help the poor blind man when He was on earth. (See John 9:1–41.) He is as willing today to accept and bless you as He was to bless the leper (see Luke 17:11–19) or to heal the paralytic (see Mark 2:1–12). Go to Him then at once, poor seeker!

Go to Him with holy confidence, for He is not in the tomb—He would be dead if He were—He is risen, living, and reigning, to answer your request! The angel bade the holy women investigate the empty tomb, but almost immediately after, he gave them a commission to perform on their Lord's behalf. (See Matthew 28:6–7.) Now, if any seeker here has been comforted by the thought that Christ lives to save, let him do as the angel said—let him go and tell others of the good news that he has heard. It is the great means for propagating our holy faith, that all who have learned it should teach it. We have not some ministers set apart to whom is reserved the sole right of teaching in the Christian church! We have no belief in a clergy and a laity!

Believers, you are all God's clerics—all of you! As many of you as believe in Christ are God's clergy and bound to serve Him according to your abilities. Many members there are in the body, but every member has its office—and there is no member in the body of Christ which is to be idle, because, indeed, it cannot do what the Head can do. The foot has its place and the hand its duty, as well as the tongue and the eyes. (See 1 Corinthians 12:12–31.) O you who have learned of Jesus, keep not the blessed secret to yourselves! Today, in some way or other, I pray you make known that Jesus Christ is risen! Pass the watchword round, as the ancient Christians did! On the first day of the week, they said to one another, "*The* LORD *is risen indeed*" (Luke 24:34).

If any ask you what you mean by it, you will then be able to tell them the whole of the gospel, for this is the essence of the gospel—that Jesus Christ died for our sins and rose again the third day, according to the Scriptures. (See 1 Corinthians 15:3–4). He died the Substitute for us criminals! He rose the Representative of us pardoned sinners! He died that our sins might die and lives again that our souls may live! Diligently invite others to come and trust Jesus. Tell them that there is life for the dead in a look at Jesus crucified! Tell them that that look is a matter of the soul! Tell them it is a simple confidence! Tell them that none ever did confide in Christ and were cast away! Tell them what you have felt as the result of your trusting Jesus, and who can tell? Many disciples may be added to His church, a risen Savior will be glorified, and you will be comforted by what you have seen!

The Lord follow these feeble words with His own blessing, for Christ's sake. Amen.

ABOUT THE AUTHOR

Charles Haddon Spurgeon was born on June 19, 1834, at Kelvedon, Essex, England, the firstborn of eight surviving children. His parents were committed Christians, and his father was a preacher. Spurgeon was converted in 1850 at the age of fifteen. He began to help the poor and to hand out tracts, and was known as "The Boy Preacher."

His next six years were eventful. He preached his first sermon at the age of sixteen. At age eighteen, he became the pastor of Waterbeach Baptist Chapel, preaching in a barn. Spurgeon preached over six hundred times before he reached the age of twenty. By 1854 he was well-known and was asked to become the pastor of New Park Street Chapel in London. In 1856, Spurgeon married Susannah Thompson; they had twin sons, both of whom later entered the ministry.

Spurgeon's compelling sermons and lively preaching style drew multitudes of people, and many came to Christ. Soon, the crowds had grown so large that they blocked the narrow streets near the church. Services eventually had to be held in rented halls, and he often preached to congregations of more than ten thousand. The Metropolitan Tabernacle was built in 1861 to accommodate the large numbers of people.

Spurgeon published over two thousand sermons, which were so popular that they literally sold by the ton. At one point his sermons sold twenty-five thousand copies every week. An 1870 edition of the English magazine *Vanity Fair* called him an "original and powerful preacher...honest, resolute, sincere; lively, entertaining." He appealed constantly to his hearers to move on in the Christian faith, to allow the Lord to minister to them individually, and to be used of God to win the lost to Christ. His sermons were scripturally inspiring and highlighted with flashes of spontaneous and delightful humor. The prime minister of England, members of the royal family, and Florence Nightingale, among others, went to hear him preach. Spurgeon preached to an estimated ten million people throughout his life. Not surprisingly, he is called the "Prince of Preachers."

In addition to his powerful preaching, Spurgeon founded and supported charitable outreaches, including educational institutions. His pastors' college, which is still in existence today, taught nearly nine hundred students in Spurgeon's time. He also founded the famous Stockwell Orphanage.

In his later years, Spurgeon often publicly disagreed with the emergence of modern biblical criticism that led the believer away from a total dependence on the Word of God.

Charles Spurgeon died at Menton, France, in 1892, leaving a legacy of writings to the believer who seeks to know the Lord Jesus more fully.